Chester G. Starr

THE ROMAN EMPIRE

27 B.C. - A.D. 476

A Study in Survival

The Roman Empire
27 B.C.–A.D. 476

The Roman Empire
27 B.C.–A.D. 476

A Study in Survival

CHESTER G. STARR

NEW YORK   OXFORD
Oxford University Press
1982

Copyright © 1982 by Oxford University Press, Inc.

LIBRARY OF CONGRESS CATALOGING IN PUBLICATION DATA

Starr, Chester G., 1914–
  The Roman Empire, 27 B.C.–A.D. 476.

  Bibliography: p.
  Includes index.
  1. Rome—History—Empire—30 B.C.–476 A.D.
I. Title. II. Title: Roman Empire, 27 BC–AD 476.
DG270.S67   937′.06   81–22310
ISBN 0–19–503129–6   AACR2
ISBN 0–19–503130–X (pbk.)

Printing (last digit): 9 8 7 6 5 4 3 2 1

Printed in the United States of America

To
Elmer and Ruth Ellis
in friendship

Preface

As the title page and introduction indicate, this work is primarily a study of structure, only secondarily of events. From any point of view, however, the Roman Empire is fascinating as the longest period of political unity in Western civilization and also as an institution with a remarkably intricate constitution and interplay of forces.

For many ideas I am indebted to other students, but I have deliberately restricted notes to suggest the origins of quotations and specific, usually statistical facts. I am grateful to my colleagues for awarding me the Hudson research chair for 1980–81.

Ann Arbor, Michigan   Chester G. Starr
Good Friday 1982

Plates and Maps

Contents

The Roman Empire
27 B.C.–A.D. 476

Introduction

The best-known fact about the Roman Empire is that it declined and fell. Insofar as this great "event" did occur—later we shall see why quotation marks are needed—it has proven to be a very useful symbol in the modern world. Conservative economists or social observers can parade it as a dread but clear warning that the same will happen to us under the crushing burdens of heavy taxation, state socialism, or moral degeneration, unless we reverse the irreversible. Outwardly objective scholars are more inclined to explore why the Decline and Fall took place, but they too may be pleading a special case. Thus, for example, the two agronomists who wrote a book on topsoil throughout history: the Romans eventually exhausted *their* topsoil, with dire consequences.

My concern here is not primarily with the Decline and Fall, for that may rightly be said to have been inevitable. All states must eventually disintegrate or so change as to be really new structures. Scipio Aemilianus had wept in 146 B.C. as he watched burning Carthage, the old, now crushed foe of Rome, for he feared the same fate for Rome "when he reflected on the fate of all things human."[1]

The Roman Empire, after all, was an impossibility. Geographically it stretched, at its peak, a thousand miles from southern Scotland to southern Egypt; on the east Roman frontiers lay in the sun-baked upper plains along the Euphrates River and on the west stopped only at the Atlantic Ocean. This huge block was larger than the whole earth today, if measured in terms of ancient communications and transportation. Couriers averaged 50

miles per day, and ships generally attained at best half this figure.[2] An ancient orator exaggerated only in reasonable degree
when he asserted that "for one starting from Rome, there was an
outward journey of months and years if he wished to see the walls
of soldiers and true fortifications on the frontiers."[3]

Economically as well the Empire appears an impossibility. Almost all its population—about 90 per cent—was agriculturally
based and in most areas produced very little more than was
needed for the farmers' subsistence.[4] Yet the inhabitants of the
Empire, who may have numbered about 50 million, supported a
standing professional army and navy of some 300,000 men, the
largest and most expensive military force the world had ever
seen; even demographically this was a remarkable achievement.
The emperors built palaces and temples on a lavish scale; the
physical remains of the once-bustling cities from Pompeii to Syria
and north Africa are still impressive. Somehow the humble
shoulders of the imperial peasantry bore these burdens and did
so for centuries without serious unrest.

Psychologically and politically the Roman Empire was equally
implausible, for in constitutional principles its political structure
perpetuated the rules and customs of the Roman Republic. True
hereditary succession was impossible, for the formal powers of the
magistrates of state came from the *populus Romanus* or citizen
body, acting through its assemblies, which had ultimate, unfet-
tered authority at least after the Hortensian law of 287 B.C. On
the death of an "emperor," thus, his powers lapsed back into the
hands of the people, and only by its grant could his successor
theoretically occupy a position which he held de facto. Yet as the
historian Appian observed of Caesar, the man who in reality
ended the Republic, "he strengthened, systematized, and secured
[power] and, while preserving the form and name of the republic, made himself the absolute master of all." His successors, continues Appian, are not called kings but rather *imperatores,* "but
in truth they are kings over everything." This ambiguity Ortega y
Gasset described as producing a society "constitutionally sick and
defective," i.e., the Roman Empire was essentially illegitimate
and not a structure of law.[5] Such a view, as we shall see in look-

ing at the career of Augustus, who stabilized the Empire, is extreme, yet deliberate ambiguity does remain.

Nonetheless this vast extent of land and sea formed a conscious political entity which endured for century upon century, conventionally running from 27 B.C. to A.D. 476. And across this half millennium much survived outwardly unchanged. The last Roman emperor in the west, upon forced abdication, was exiled to a villa on the Bay of Naples which had been built by the late Roman Republican general Lucullus; a pretender to the throne in Constantinople late in the fourth century after Christ raised the battle cry of "redivision of the land, abolition of debts, the happiness of the time of Cronus and Rhea"—popular demands which ran back in Greek history at least to the fourth century B.C.[6]

Looked at in this light, the Roman Empire is a fascinating and important historical puzzle: why did it survive so long despite its impossibility? The simplistic rejoinder that it actually was already in existence by the Late Republic does not wipe away the problem, for the Mediterranean world came very close to dissolution in the civil wars which produced the dominance of Augustus and the establishment of a relatively permanent order. A study such as the present one must lead us into many interwoven aspects of the political, military, and economic history of the Empire, not all of which are easily penetrated; in some areas the emperors preferred secrecy, and in others our sources are not sufficiently interested to give us the information that modern students would wish. Although intellectual and spiritual aspects of the tale are certainly important, I shall refer to them only in passing, both to avoid undue complication of the story and also because I discussed this side in another work some years ago. Even with these limitations the effort to account for the long survival of the Empire is much worth making for itself and as an exploration of basic factors in the development of mankind.

Modern historians have great difficulty in describing the Roman Empire both in time and in space. In character of civilization the provinces were far from uniform, nor were all its centuries serene and orderly. Often students of the Empire have resigned themselves to discussing only its first two centuries, which are reasonably tidy, or have limited their scope to that Greco-Roman upper crust which produced almost all our literary evidence; but both restrictions seriously blinker our understanding of the strengths in the imperial system.

In another respect as well there are difficulties. Theodor Mommsen once observed, "History, the struggle of necessity and liberty, is a moral problem,"[7] a truth illustrated by the current dichotomy in evaluations of the Empire. On the one side are those scholars who move from Tacitus' famous dictum, "They make a desert and call it peace," to condemn the Empire as a purely exploitive structure. This view is amusingly but viciously put by a popular writer, "Rome was not the first state of organized gangsterdom, nor was it the last; but it was the only one that managed to bamboozle posterity into an almost universal admiration."[8] Until recently, in truth, almost all students—and with more justice—have endorsed Gibbon's judgment that at least the first two centuries of the Empire were the happiest era in human history down to his own day. The ancient paeans to peace and prosperity are not purely rhetorical flourishes.

How is one to proceed to uncover the "structures," to use a term prominent in recent French historical thought, or the institutions and attitudes of mind which could permit the Empire to survive some five centuries? The textbook approach is to describe developments chronologically in terms of the reigns of the successive emperors, whose individual peccadilloes bulk large in many of our written sources, such as Suetonius, Tacitus, and Dio Cassius; in this scheme the city of Rome occupies the center of the stage, often to such an extent that the provinces lie dimly in the background. One recent scholar has argued that, on the contrary, true understanding of the nature of the Empire can be attained only "by starting from the provinces and looking inward."[9] To pursue this line of attack seriously would put us in danger of losing sight of the forest in describing individual trees (or provinces), but the point most certainly needs to be kept in mind that forces could flow into Rome as well as outward. A straight chronological narrative, moreover, is not the best way to disentangle and view clearly basic aspects of the significant institutions; the most useful approach is an analytical one, and the characteristics of individual rulers will alas appear only occasionally.

In the first six chapters we shall move from the emperor himself outward through the classes and organs of the imperial administration, thereafter shall turn to local government and life, and then to the armed forces. These chapters, which will describe the consolidation of the pillars on which the Empire rested, will limit their scope to the era 27 B.C.–A.D. 211, almost two and one-half centuries, as forming a coherent unit, the height of the Early Empire. By including the reign of Septimius Severus I vary from the usual periodization, but Septimius Severus himself firmly claimed inheritance from the Antonine emperors of the later second century even though his fiscal severity and emphasis on the army presage the third century.

After 211 change becomes more evident, at times chaotic, though the forces and forms which held the Empire together continued to be effective for another two centuries; this later period will be the subject of the last two chapters. Temporally my allocation of space may seem unjust to the later centuries of the Empire, which are fascinating in themselves as transitional from ancient to medieval times, but to repeat a point which cannot be overstressed: my objective is an analytical rather than a simple chronological survey of imperial history. In covering such a range of time and aspects it is often necessary to be general—though not thereby abstract—but an essential attribute of history is the support of generalization at appropriate points by engaging, specific illustrations.

Notes

1. Polybius 38. 22, who was present at the scene.
2. L. Friedländer, *Roman Life and Manners under the Early Roman Empire,* 1, (New York, 1908), pp. 280–81, 285–86; M. Amit, "Les Moyens de communication et la défense de l'Empire romain," *Parola del Passato,* 20 (1965), pp. 207–22.
3. Aristides, *On Rome* 80 (adapted).
4. A. H. M. Jones, *The Later Roman Empire, 284–602* (Oxford, 1964), pp. 464–65, 769–73.

5. Appian, *Roman History,* Preface 6; J. Ortega y Gasset, *An Interpretation of Universal History* (New York, 1973), p. 83.
6. Themistius, *Oration* 7. 91C.
7. Theodor Mommsen, *History of Rome,* 4 (New York, 1895), p. 246.
8. Tacitus, *Agricola* 30, a statement not even verbally original with Tacitus (cf. Pliny, *Natural History* 6. 182); the concept appears also in Curtius Rufus, *Alexander* 9. 2. 24. Petr Beckmann, *A History of Pi* (Boulder, Colorado, 1970), p. 52.
9. F. Millar, *Journal of Roman Studies,* 56 (1966), p. 166.

CHAPTER I

Augustus

One day in August 30 B.C. a man whom we know as Augustus stood at Alexander's tomb and looked down on the embalmed body of the great conqueror. At that point the man was still called Gaius Iulius Caesar Octavianus—Octavian for short—or sometimes Caesar the Younger. He had entered Alexandria without opposition on the first day of the month; his defeated opponents Antony and then Cleopatra had removed themselves by suicide.

It would be absorbing to know what thoughts passed through Octavian's mind. At the age of 20 Alexander had become king of Macedonia, a state made powerful by his father Philip. Octavian had begun *his* career at 18, a schoolboy whose only asset was the fact that as the grandnephew of Caesar he was the sole male relative of the dead dictator. Now he was a master of 60 legions, 900 warships, and all the Roman world.

What would or could he do with his power? Two men in the past 50 years had become masters of Rome by force, but from them Octavian could learn only by observing their mistakes. Sulla, a conservative, had concentrated formal authority in the hands of the Senate, a body of some 600 aristocrats which theoretically gave advice to the magistrates but in practice established and supervised public policy; within a decade of Sulla's reorganization the Senate had lost its dominant position through the interplay of internal factionalism. Caesar himself thought Sulla a fool for yielding his mastery and planned to continue a blatantly open rule; unlike Sulla, who had ruthlessly eliminated his opponents, Caesar pursued a clement, forgiving policy and had been rewarded by assassination.

Certainly much needed restoration or improvement in the Roman world, for the last century of the Republic had been turbulent. The wars of the era were essentially a struggle of individuals and factions for control of the state, rather than a crusade for a great principle, but the unrest affected all the Mediterranean world. There was no certainty of life for aristocrats or even for common folk, caught in Rome by gang warfare, on the seas by piracy, on land by the breakdown of order due to wandering slaves, brigands, and external invasions or by the great drafts to man the warring armies.

Nor was there certainty of property. Men of moderate means, like the poet Virgil, as well as the wealthy lost their lands without compensation in the expropriations required to reward the veterans of the civil wars; the coinage was unstable and limited in quantity; taxes were imposed arbitrarily and on some occasions for 10 years at once. Men's minds were attuned to change and upheaval; any adventurer could fan up supporters swiftly. In such an age militarism seemed endemic.

Now it was Octavian's responsibility to secure his own position and to set up permanent dams and dikes against this spirit of chaos. The responsibility he consciously recognized; as he once stated in an edict,

> May it be my privilege to establish the State in a firm and secure position, and enjoy therefrom the rewards of which I am ambitious, that of being called the author of the best possible government, and of carrying with me when I die the hope that the foundations which I have laid for the State will remain unshaken.[1]

His hope was fulfilled; the result was the structure which we call the Roman Empire. His reforms artfully, at times unconsciously, capitalized on the inherited strengths of the Roman world; they also incorporated some dangerous weaknesses which were to plague the Empire for centuries.

The Political Settlement

Octavian had risen to power in the years after Caesar's murder in 44 B.C. essentially by the use of military force, beginning with Caesar's veterans, and by the skillful exercise of a cold, calculating mind. His initial program had been simply vengeance for his great-uncle, and he and his associates had listed for execution 300 senators and 2000 equestrians, including Cicero. Already by 41–40, however, he had begun to discover that ruthlessness was not a good base for lasting power; as the historian Dio Cassius observed, he could force men but not thereby gain their hearts. Across the decade of the 30s, as a consequence, he delicately shifted his stance so as to appear the supporter of old Roman ways and restorer of order in Italy. The runaway slaves in the fleet of Sextus Pompey, one of his early opponents, were returned to their masters in 36, and at that time he recounted his exploits in speeches to the Senate and people and attempted to justify his acts from the beginning; on the same occasion he burned all the vehement pamphlets which he had issued during the war against Sextus Pompey. The spirit of 36 was duly immortalized in a gilded image of Octavian erected in the Forum on a column and bearing the inscription, "Peace, long disturbed, he re-established on land and sea."[2] Caesar the Younger even jettisoned the memory of Caesar the Elder to the hatred of the Roman aristocracy, for Caesar was to be little stressed thereafter; rather Octavian came to praise Caesar's ideological foe, Cato the Younger, as a model of rectitude and civic justice.

From this point forward Octavian's policy was built around the principles of moderation, peace, outwardly constitutional conduct, and the domination of a conjoined Italy and Rome in the Mediterranean world. His conversion won for him the adhesion of powerful groups. Many of the senators came to his side; although no public opinion polls exist to measure Octavian's popularity in Italy, his backing there certainly increased rapidly after 36. The poets Virgil and Horace give us actual examples of this shift, for both abandoned doubt or hostility to accept Octavian's policies in the 30s.

Eventually Octavian dared to turn against his erstwhile partner Antony and in an unparalleled propaganda campaign assailed his opponent as falling away from things Roman for the fleshpots of the Orient, embodied in the siren Cleopatra. Octavian raised his preparations for war almost to the level of a crusade; Italy paid him heavy, extraordinary taxes, and its inhabitants in 32 swore "of their own will" an oath to support him. Relying on this evidence of loyalty, Octavian gave up the despotic powers he had extorted in 43 and posed for the next few years as leader by universal desire, a position which was to underly his later recon-struction of the Roman government. His general Agrippa skill-fully maneuvered the forces of Antony and Cleopatra into a hope-less position on the west coast of Greece and on September 3, 31, easily defeated the enemy navy at Actium.

After his return from Alexandria to Rome Octavian moved de-liberately toward formal reorganization of the Roman constitu-tion. Always his motto was "make haste slowly" (*festina lente*), and he was fortunate in having 44 more years after 30 B.C. in which to follow this principle. Unlike Caesar he always main-tained a bodyguard—a wise step inasmuch as at least five down-right plots and other individual efforts at assassination were to occur in his lifetime.

By 28–27 he was ready to eliminate many of the illegalities of the civil wars. The most visible ceremony took place on January 13, 27, when he made a speech in the Senate formally proclaim-ing the restoration of constitutional government, and in particu-lar returning control of the provinces to the jurisdiction of the Senate. In return the Senate voted him an oak wreath "for saving the citizens" (*ob civis servatos*)—a token which he was to employ often on his coinage—and ordered the doorposts of his house decorated with laurel in honor of his victories. After a two-day interval partly caused by religious reasons the Senate met again on the sixteenth and accepted the change of name which he had decided upon: Imperator Caesar, son of the god (Caesar), Augus-tus. Probably at this meeting it gave him control for 10 years over the most warlike or threatened provinces, and either then or in the next year set up a golden shield emblazoned with his four cardinal virtues: *virtus, clementia, iustitia, pietas*—terms which had far wider, more complex meanings than their English derivatives.

This, however, did not end Augustus' tinkering with his own position. In 23 he fell seriously ill and gave up the consulship, to which he had been elected each year; further changes took place in 19 and even thereafter. In the end Augustus could proclaim that he surpassed other citizens only in his "authority" (*auctoritas*, which we might better call "prestige") but as "first citizen" (*princeps*) held a bundle of constitutional powers disassociated from Republican magistracies. These included the tribunician power, by which he could pose as protector of the ordinary Roman citizen and also veto any action in Rome; the *imperium*, or power to command armies; the proconsular *imperium*, renewed every 5 or 10 years, over about half the provinces (the Senate appointing proconsuls or propraetors each year to the other, senatorial provinces); the *imperium maius*, or "greater *imperium*," by which he could legally interfere in or control the administration of those senatorial provinces; and sundry other honors and religious posts. Beneath the surface he was absolute master, but in outward guise he—and others—could celebrate the resuscitation of constitutional order.

Augustus' reorganization was shrewdly built on the customs and principles of the Republic but implicit within it were enduring problems for the Empire. We shall look at these more fully in the next chapter; at this point it will suffice to observe in a system deliberately engineered to be imprecise in theory each new *princeps* had to establish for himself how he actually would operate, and that if a ruler wished to be tyrannical there was no real check save assassination. Also on the death of an emperor, to repeat a point made in the Introduction, the constitutional powers by which he could govern and control all aspects of the government went back to the people so that true hereditary succession was impossible. Yet Augustus clearly intended that his system should continue: he had eventually succeeded his great-uncle; so too following *principes* should come from his own family.

Here biological accident caused him much grief. He had had

a daughter Julia by his first wife (Scribonia); his second wife, Livia, had had two sons (Tiberius and Drusus) by her previous husband—she had in fact been pregnant when Augustus passionately took her away from that husband. But Augustus and Livia together could not produce a child; Livia did conceive once, but aborted early. An American may well think of the marriage of George Washington and Martha Custis, the latter of whom at any rate was fertile; American history too might well have been different if Washington had had a mature, able son at the time of his presidency.

All Augustus could do was to raise up collateral relatives as potential successors or marry off his daughter Julia to one husband after another, first to his general Agrippa, then on Agrippa's death to his stepson Tiberius. Grandchildren were duly produced, but they too died save for the apparently aimless ne'er-do-well Agrippa Postumus. Eventually, but reluctantly, Augustus settled on Tiberius, who took over the Principate on Augustus' death in A.D. 14.

Beyond establishing his own position Augustus had also to face the problems of strengthening the administration of the Empire. Nowadays there is a common tendency to call the last years of the Republic the Roman Revolution. Since the term "revolution" may mean many things, its usage here may be accepted provided one does not visualize the Roman Revolution as a great social whirlwind, rising suddenly and fraught with ideological drive. The upheaval connoted by the phrase was very directly political in nature. Naturally it was influenced by the economic, social, and intellectual changes in the Mediterranean world following the Roman conquests; but the primary force leading to the great alterations of the last century B.C., to simplify the highly complicated, was the necessity of adjusting ineffective political machinery to the governance of a Mediterranean-wide empire. Closely linked with this issue, but logically on a secondary plane, was the enlargement of the governing class.

Augustus could not do everything himself, though the picture from our sources is of a man who worked very hard day and night; for one thing he was sickly by nature and had to husband his energies. Machiavelli commented in *Il Principe* that "king-doms known to history have been governed in two ways: either by a prince and his servants . . . or by a prince and by barons who hold their positions not by favor of the ruler but by antiquity of blood."³ Augustus skillfully employed *both* methods concurrently; his personal staff and some of the financial officials were imperial slaves and freedmen, while the prestigious posts in the army and provinces were given to reliable aristocrats. Thenceforth the latter were more carefully supervised than had been possible in the breakdown of the Republic; a well-known set of decrees shows Augustus using his *imperium maius* to intervene in the government of the senatorial province of Cyrene. Still, inefficiency, arrogance, and corruption were not to disappear. In a later chapter we shall examine more carefully the elaboration of governmental machinery in the Empire, but two points must be stressed here. First, Augustus firmly consolidated in public life the class distinctions which had grown more pronounced in the Late Republic; and second, he expanded the opportunities of the equestrian class, a lower level of Roman aristocracy than the senators, and of the leading magnates in the Italian cities to enter the imperial hierarchy.

As Tacitus bitingly summed up the changes, "Rome accepted the *princeps* and peace." To some degree it did so perforce, for the memory of the young Octavian did not vanish; in his rise he had killed more senators and equestrians than did all his successors for two centuries to come. Even as Augustus he still had a secret police and informers; political trials of occasional dissidents brought exile, execution, or suicide in desperation; laws on violence (*de vi*) and on treason (*de maiestate*) were mighty tools to strike down opposition within a legal framework by which an ambitious man might be taught "not to exalt his mind above the mass of mankind."⁴

Yet one virtue paraded on his golden shield was "clemency," and Augustus sought to project that virtue in practice as far as his own safety permitted. The biographer Suetonius gives numerous examples of his refusal to follow up scurrilous pamphlets as well as his toleration of opposition in the Senate (though he had far more often to check its adulation). Two illustrations will suffice. One concerns Timagenes, who made hostile remarks about Augustus and his family which were much repeated in Rome. Finally Augustus banned Timagenes from his house; when his fellow historian Asinius Pollio gave Timagenes a home Augustus only observed that Pollio was housing a menagerie. Pollio sought to excuse himself and offered to expel Timagenes if Augustus so ordered, but the reply was, "Do you think that I would do this when it was *I* who restored the friendship between you?" Then there was the case of a senator who in his cups expressed the hope that Augustus would not return from a journey which he was about to make. Some fellow guests carefully noted the utterance, and on the following morning the contrite culprit rushed to the Forum to beg Augustus' pardon; the emperor had to prove his forgiveness by granting the senator a large gift of money and ruefully hoped that similar events would not force him to keep on with such generosity.[5] Outward urbanity and surface respect for legality by Augustus combined with weariness of chaos on the part of the aristocracy to produce political stabilization.

The Augustan Peace

Tacitus, as just noted, couples *princeps* and peace, a junction which Augustus himself fostered in his coinage and in the erection of the magnificently sculptured Altar of Augustan Peace (see Plate I). In Virgil's poetry, in the Forum dedication of 36 already cited, and in an abundance of other evidence a cry for peace wells up from both the upper classes and the depths of the Empire; Augustus boasted that he had closed the doors of the shrine of Janus three times to symbolize that the realm was at peace. Yet here particularly modern meanings of a word may mislead us seriously, for *pax* in the Roman world had a far more positive connotation than our equivalent. To the Romans peace meant "world empire with security from outside interference, law and order within."[6]

After the victory at Actium Augustus swiftly reduced the swollen ranks of his army and navy by establishing military colonies; those in Asia Minor long remained Latin strongholds, at least for official actions, in a largely Greek environment. This

I Mother Earth. A relief from the Altar of Augustan Peace in Rome bears children, grain and fruits, and domestic animals—a majestic result of Augustus' restoration of order and peace in the Mediterranean world. Moretti, *Ara Pacis Augustae*

time, as a result of the spoils from Egypt, he could afford to compensate those whose lands were thus used. Agrippa was assigned the task of establishing a permanent and coherent army and navy to defend and expand the Empire; this important operation was essentially completed by 16 B.C., and the new system, while derived from the past, was to be dominant for the next two centuries.

At least in principle the military forces consisted of long-term volunteers, legionaries serving 16, then 20 years; auxiliaries and sailors serving 25 or 26 years. The army was split into two types of units: legions of citizens as the infantry backbone, and auxiliary units of non-citizens comprising cavalry, slingers, and other lighter-armed troops. Upon discharge legionaries received a bonus in cash or land; to meet these expenses Augustus endowed a military treasury (*aerarium militare*) which was thereafter fed by a 5 per cent tax on inheritances, even of small amounts, by heirs not closely connected to the deceased and 1 per cent on auction sales.[7]

In a later chapter we shall look more closely at this military structure to assess its weaknesses and strengths in defending the Empire across its first two centuries; Agrippa's solution was a very expensive one, for the military item was by far the heaviest in the state budget. Augustus also encouraged internal military disarmament to reduce dangers of rebellion. The question remained, what if the army could not hold the frontiers? Or equally important as far as the emperor himself was concerned, how could he make certain that the troops were not incited to revolt?

At the time, however, Augustus and Agrippa had created a magnificent fighting machine, and there was no doubt that it was meant to be used. From the fourth century B.C. onward the Republic had steadily extended its sway over the Mediterranean world; down to the time of Augustus there were no true frontiers, only halting points of greater or lesser duration in this expansion. The aristocrats who dominated the Republic had had two public functions: to gain major posts of state (a competitive activity which still caused trouble to Augustus) and to secure glory for their clans by military victory. Augustus himself erected a statue to Victoria in the Senate House and was the first Roman depicted on coins as holding a globe on which stood a winged victory (see Plate II). Here too, even so, Augustus was patient and moved deliberately; he likened fighting a war to fishing with a golden fishhook in reference both to risks and to costs as against profits of conquest.[8]

In two areas Augustus consciously decided not to fight. Stretching eastward from the Roman province of Syria was the vast Parthian realm, the only civilized state on Rome's borders; and Augustus saw no gain in challenging it (see Map 1). Yet there was a delicate matter of honor inasmuch as the Parthians held several eagles, or legionary standards, captured in two Roman defeats during the Late Republic. By diplomacy, backed by threats, Augustus won the peaceful return of the standards, a success which he proudly illustrated on coins by showing a kneeling Parthian ruler; the neighboring minor kingdom of Armenia "I could have made into a province but preferred to follow the custom of our ancestors" by installing Tigranes as king.[9] The other region he ignored was Britain, though it had been invaded twice by Caesar. To justify this exclusion Augustus argued that the costs of conquest would overbalance possible revenues, an argument preserved in comments by Strabo—and a wise one which his successors unfortunately failed to accept. In his own account of his deeds, the *Res Gestae,* Augustus also noted the submission of British chieftains to his majesty, which made invasion less necessary.

Before turning to his primary field of military activity Augustus sought to tidy up two peripheral zones. One was the Red Sea, where Cornelius Gallus led a joint military-naval force in 25 and 24 B.C. to secure control over its eastern coast; this effort was thwarted by the heat and difficult geography, and Augustus pursued it no further. In Spain the Romans held only the eastern and southern coasts and some parts of the interior; ever since this annexation after the Second Punic War Spain had been unruly and often a serious threat to Roman peace. Augustus himself came to Spain in 27 and directed extensive military operations which resulted in the pacification of the whole Iberian peninsula.

All this was preliminary to his expansion of Roman rule in the center of Europe and the Balkans. Tiberius and Drusus, his step-

II Peace and the Conquered. Two scenes from a silver cup found on the slopes of Mount Vesuvius, which illustrate the submission of conquered German peoples to Augustus. In one scene he is sitting on the official campstool of a magistrate, dressed in a toga (contrast the military garb of Plate III), and Venus is offering him a winged figure of Victory. *Monuments Piot 5 (1901)*

sons, cooperated in a pincers attack in 15 which netted Noricum and the Vindelicii, modern Austria and Switzerland. Thereafter Tiberius and other leaders conquered Pannonia, essentially modern Yugoslavia, in 12 through 10, and Drusus expanded Roman rule from the Rhine to the Elbe in campaigns from 12 down to his death in 9. Other generals were active in the lower Balkans, extending Roman power to the Danube.

Here arose one of those intricate but little historical problems which suddenly illuminate a great deal about major forces and attitudes. The general M. Licinius Crassus personally slew in duel an opposing king and claimed the rare Roman honor of dedicating *spolia opima* on the Capitoline hill. This claim was denied on the grounds that Crassus was acting as a deputy for Augustus in his proconsular *imperium;* when it was pointed out that one of the three previous dedicants, Cossus, had been only a military tribune, a fortunate antiquarian discovery was made which proved Cossus to have been consul. Legalism nicely triumphed; Augustus might be forced to allow Roman aristocrats to gain glory in war but not that much. Crassus was granted a triumph, but "in the ensuing years his services were no longer required."[10] No general outside the imperial house ever got a formal triumph in Rome after 19 B.C.; the dust and blood of battle and march might be the lot of others, but the emperor claimed the glory.

Under the auspices of Augustus Roman eagles advanced triumphantly eastward and northward in Europe, and as far as one can tell Augustus had no intention of halting their progress; Virgil had had Jupiter proclaim in the *Aeneid,* "I have given Rome rule without end."[11] Accepted geographical views also encouraged advance by assigning central Europe a much smaller area than it actually occupies. A temporary delay did take place while Augustus proposed to deal with the Marcomanni who occupied Bohemia, but unfortunately in 6 B.C. Tiberius withdrew in virtual exile to Rhodes, piqued by Augustus' favor to his own grandsons. Lacking any strong and safe leader—always to be a problem in imperial history—Augustus engaged in only minor feints until A.D. 4, when Tiberius returned to public life (the grandsons Gaius and Lucius now being dead).

The delay proved decisive for the next five centuries. Tiberius

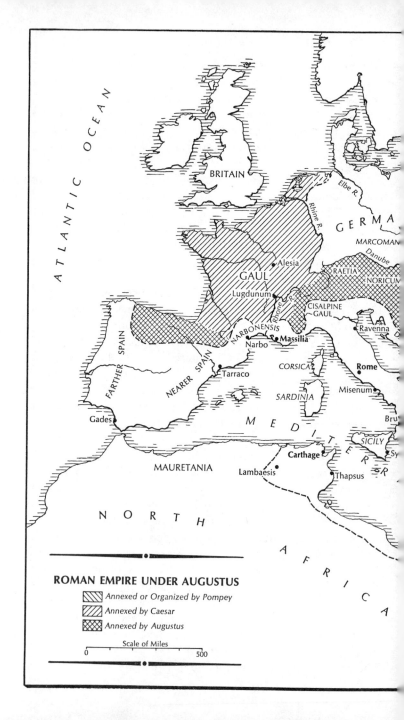

ROMAN EMPIRE UNDER AUGUSTUS

Annexed or Organized by Pompey

Annexed by Caesar

Annexed by Augustus

Scale of Miles

0   500

did advance again to the Elbe by A.D. 6, and a concentric attack began on the Marcomanni—only to be halted abruptly on news of a great rebellion in Pannonia. Putting this down required three years in a costly war, for "but very little booty was taken." Immediately thereafter the Roman governor of Germany, Varus, was trapped and killed along with his three legions, and Roman power east of the Rhine was shattered. Augustus, over 70 by this time, roamed his mansion and dashed his head against doors, crying out "Varus, give me back my legions."[12] Even replacing the lost manpower in minor degree required drafting veterans and freedmen since not enough citizens would volunteer.

Tiberius restored order on the Rhine, but Augustus made no effort to resume the advance; he is reported, though probably erroneously, to have advised Tiberius as successor not to expand the Empire farther. In any case masses of Germanic tribes were left free of the blessings of Roman peace, and at a much later date became the visible agents in ending Roman rule in the western provinces—but could the Roman advance truly have swallowed up all Europe? More significant, and ultimately as dangerous, was the fact that Rome was slowly acquiring true frontiers, a process which was to become more evident in the passive reign of Tiberius even though some annexations were to be made over the next century. All in all, Augustus conquered more territory than any other single individual in Roman history, and opened vital land connections between the western European provinces and the eastern frontiers, a step which much facilitated defensive strategy during the Empire.

Economic and Social Reforms

Political and military problems were certainly the areas to which Augustus devoted the most continuous and at times anguished attention. Economic issues, which bulk large in the eyes of modern statesmen, concerned him as little as they did any ancient politician. There was in antiquity no concept of economic growth, no measurement of gross national product (impossible anyway in a society which existed largely on the subsistence level), or for that matter no direct study of economics for itself. Nonetheless Augustus did have some awareness of state revenues and expenditures and their effects on economic life as a whole. By coining the gold and silver in the royal treasury of Egypt "he made ready money so abundant that the rate of interest fell and the value of real estate rose greatly,"[13] and at least twice he had to discuss in the Senate the best means of funding the *aerarium militare;* throughout his life he maintained, and left to his successor, a balance sheet of the Empire. A modern scholar notes in him "the hard realism, the lack of chivalry, the caution and the parsimony"—all true, yet in keeping his economic house in order Augustus had sufficient surplus to permit lavish gifts to the citizens of Rome and to finance a great building program, parts of which are summarized in appendices to his *Res Gestae.*[14]

In the provinces military camps, roads, triumphal arches, and other structures rose at public and private expense as the Roman world regained stability and prosperity after the civil wars; this revival was particularly notable in the Greek East, which had directly borne most of the brunt of those wars. Many of the urban buildings and even whole new cities celebrated the deeds and name of Augustus; in Rome itself he more directly saw to it that architectural activity was interwoven with his achievements so that "the majesty of the empire was expressed through the eminent dignity of its public buildings."[15] Recently it has even been argued that Augustus had an enormous planning scheme for the whole Campus Martius, centering on an obelisk and embracing a circle twice as large as St. Peter's Square today, along which his massive mausoleum, the Altar of Augustan Peace, and other edifices were deliberately placed.

Beside the Roman Forum he erected another forum which deftly illustrates the place which he sought for himself. The Forum of Augustus was focussed on the temple of Mars the Avenger, whose statue was placed between those of Venus the Begetter (ancestress of the Julian clan) and of the deified Caesar; as the focus of Rome's military glory the Senate met here to vote triumphs, and recaptured standards were enshrined. In front of the temple were two hemicycles on north and south for the display of statues. Augustus placed in this Valhalla effigies of the "leaders who had raised the estate of the Roman people from obscurity to greatness" and by edict announced that they were to be held as an example to himself and later *principes*.[16] Both here and in his funeral procession, where the images of the great heroes of Rome were paraded, lay an unwritten assertion that Augustus stood in the direct line of Roman statesmen and generals. Though the spirit of its builder was everywhere present in this Forum, Augustus carefully avoided his own representation until 2 B.C., when the Senate voted to erect in its center a statue of the ruler in a chariot with his new title of *pater patriae*.

In another major area Augustus supported economic activity, by providing a stable, abundant coinage in gold (*aureus*), silver (*denarius* and *quinarius*), orichalcum (brass *dupondius* and *sestertius*), and copper (*as* and *quadrans*)—one *aureus* equalled 25 *denarii,* and one *denarius* in turn was worth four *sestertii*. Always in the ancient world coinage was struck primarily for public purposes, but in the Late Republic such coins as were issued came to bear symbols of the glorious deeds of aristocratic clans. Augustus went much further, though not as far as his successors in the second century after Christ, in using the coinage to present his policies and achievements. The military and diplomatic triumphs of the reign were directly emphasized; other motifs proclaimed the importance of Augustus in safeguarding internal security. As in modern state propaganda the positive was always stressed; the Varian disaster lay in silence, but the coins of the state mint at Alexandria in A.D. 10–11 praised the "victory" won by Tiberius on the Rhenish frontier during those two years.

Whatever their public purpose, the coins could support and channel economic activity in many ways. The copper issues in particular were largely designed to pay the troops on the frontiers, whose expenditures encouraged the growth of trade and industry outward from the more civilized interior. In the last days of Augustus a group of Alexandrian merchants, just arrived in a nearby Italian port, marched to greet him, clad in white with laurel wreaths on their heads, and proclaimed, "through him they lived, through him they sailed the seas, and through him they enjoyed their liberty and their fortunes."[17]

If economic prosperity was an incidental, almost unconscious by-product of the restoration of order and the advance of the Roman legions, social reform was quite a different matter. Augustus strove more earnestly and deeply to uplift the Roman aristocracy and common citizenry than did any ancient statesman.

In part this effort emerged out of his own character. Augustus' father had died when he was a small boy, and he had been raised by his mother in a Latin hill town, far more conservative in its ways than the cosmopolitan city of Rome. Throughout his life Augustus was to retain this outlook, which was manifested in his restoration of order in the chaotic state religion and in his marked preference for classical sobriety and refinement in the arts. Socially, as a scholar has remarked recently, Augustus remained "a bit of a prude."[18]

But there was reason enough to be concerned when he examined his contemporary aristocrats. After the vehemence of the civil wars Rome experienced what in modern terms might be called a Thermidorean reaction as men and women turned away from politics to frenetic enjoyment of life and crass materialism. Although, as I commented earlier, aristocrats were by tradition expected to seek glory in war and office, Augustus had a good deal of difficulty in securing an adequate supply of governors and generals, and accordingly leaned heavily upon members of his own family. If Horace supported in majestic odes the advance of Roman arms, another Augustan poet, Propertius, could proclaim, "No one of my blood will be a soldier";[19] one Roman equestrian even cut off the thumbs of his sons so they would not have to serve in the army. Husbands could still truly cherish their wives, as is attested in the lengthy praise of a wife who saved her husband from execution in 43 B.C. and went so far, childless herself, as to offer her husband divorce so he could marry a younger wife whom she would cherish, but both could just as easily betray the marriage vows; the Greek term for "love of family" had no Latin equivalent.[20]

So Augustus found himself forced to interfere with aristocratic dissipation by a great series of laws designed to encourage simplicity of table, child-bearing, and sanctity of married life. And here he met far more open and determined opposition than in the political field. The "gentlemen of the fishponds," as Cicero had called the aristocrats of his day for their delight in breeding rare fish—Crassus had even had a pet eel for which he made a jeweled bracelet—were too deeply impregnated with the vices of luxury to be blandished back to the dull path of virtue; both Horace and Propertius expressed, though politely, their reservations about Augustus' moral reforms.[21] Once he cited his own marriage as an ideal example of the proper subordination of wife to husband, but the senators quickly backed him into a corner by probing the exact means by which he kept Livia, well known as an imperious lady, under control.

On another occasion, to illustrate the viciousness he faced, he dined with the wealthy aristocrat Vedius Pollio, who had a matched set of six cups of semi-precious material. The nervous slave assigned to pour wine for Augustus accidentally dropped and broke his cup; Vedius tossed over his shoulder the order, "Throw him to the fish [man-eating lampreys]." Augustus intervened and asked to see the other cups, which were proudly placed before him; the emperor picked them up one by one, looked at them, and tossed them on the floor.[22] Such an example might have encouraged more respectable treatment of slaves while Augustus was on hand, but did little to ameliorate the general tone of society.

This was far better reflected in the polished, amoral verse of Ovid, the most popular Roman poet in Augustus' later years. Ovid disapproved of child-bearing as making women ugly; he wrote a manual on seduction and scoffed at marriage; his praise of Augustus, though fulsome, was incongruously inserted in such places as a discussion of the games given by the ruler—where lovers might meet their mistresses. From about 20 B.C., when Ovid started to publish, Augustus endured his poetry; but finally in A.D. 8 the aged monarch struck and exiled Ovid to a dreary town on the lower Danube where men even wore trousers. Apparently Ovid was in some minor way involved in the scandals revolving about Augustus' own daughter Julia, who was also exiled and her paramour executed in the same year. The following year Augustus partially retreated in his crusade for improving the birth-rate and morals of the aristocracy, which was to continue its profligate corruption down into the reign of Nero.

The Place of Augustus

The failure of Augustus' social reforms throws into more vivid light his remarkable success in the political and military fields. Working patiently decade after decade Augustus gave the Roman world a sense of internal security based on a consciously elaborated pattern of government which embodied two principles. First came his own preeminence, and as we have seen in regard to coinage and architecture he was not bashful in stressing his own merits and achievements; no less than 150 statues and busts of the first emperor also survive (see Plate III). The second was his emphasis on outward cooperation with the Roman aristocracy, clothed in old constitutional forms; one may also add that on the local level Augustus, to ensure urban peace, favored the dominance of the rich and wellborn as against democracy. In sum, Augustus' reforms were essentially conservative in character.

Yet a fundamental ambivalence lurked below the serene surface. Clemency was one of the four virtues emblazoned on his golden shield; later rulers often advertised clemency on their coins, and Seneca was to write a lengthy essay of advice to his pupil Nero under the title *On Clemency*. But clemency was an imperial virtue, which could be withheld as well as exercised. That ambiguity was to lead to the execution or forced suicide of aristocrats for generation after generation to come; but it was also to produce the assassination of more than one tyrannical ruler.

Modern historians have evaluated Augustus in many divers ways, but until recently have tended to treat him with respect, partly because of the great triumphs of literature in the "Augustan Age." Of late, however, scholars affected by the overtly arbitrary character of government in some contemporary states have approached Augustus, as the founder of a covertly arbitrary system, with little admiration. The extent to which the Empire was or was not a regime of law will occupy us in the next chapter; here I have tried to portray the *princeps* in the round, blem-

III Augustus. This idealized statue, found in the villa of his wife Livia
outside Rome, magnificently suggests his sure mastery of the Roman
world. His breastplate has a scene of a Parthian restoring a legionary
standard captured in the Late Republic; the cupid on the dolphin refers to Augustus' descent from the goddess Venus. *Monumenti Musei e
Gallerie Pontificie*

ishes and all, not an easy task inasmuch as he learned as a very young man to wear an outward shell of studied behavior in threading his perilous way. Thereafter he became a marble statue as it were, a symbol of calm assurance, much like the dignified, reserved figure of George Washington. Nonetheless his solution of assembling essential responsibilities in the hands of one man, who could check all levels of government and direct its armies, seems not only inevitable but highly successful in binding together a fractured society. Sulla's reforms had demonstrated the incapacity of the senatorial aristocracy; Caesar's, the dangers of open absolutism. Augustus on the other hand muffled with great art the basic realities of his position; he was, in short, the most consummate politician of antiquity.

Certainly he was revered with great and genuine enthusiasm by his contemporaries both in Rome and in the provinces. In rising to the foreground as a single, unique figure Augustus had concentrated upon himself the yearnings of men for order. To this leader, more as symbol than as living creature, the subjects turned for assurance and prosperity in the material world, for a sense of security and purpose on the spiritual level. Augustus paid proper respect to the traditions of Greek culture, accepting initiation into the ancestral Eleusinian mysteries and treating Greece itself with generosity, though he did not speak Greek as fluently as did many aristocrats; in turn the Greeks in the east accepted him with relief.

For centuries they had been accustomed to formal worship of Hellenistic kings as gods on earth, under the titles of Benefactor or Savior; now they spontaneously began to offer sacrifices on behalf of the divine Augustus, initially coupled with the earlier cult of Rome. Augustus found the role of an earthly messiah useful as a way of promoting imperial unity, and to some degree encouraged the spread of worship of the emperor into western provinces—though not formally in Italy itself, even if messianic tones crept into the poetry of Horace and Virgil. For full intensity, however, one must turn to such sources as this decree by the province of Asia about A.D. 15 which begins:

> Whereas eternal and deathless Nature has vouchsafed to men, as
> the greatest good and bringer of overwhelming benefactions, the

emperor Augustus; the father who gives us happy life; the savior of
all mankind in common whose provident care has not only fulfilled
but even surpassed the hopes of all; for both land and sea are at
peace, the cities are teeming with the blessings of concord, plenty,
and respect for the law, and the culmination and harvest of all good
things bring fair hopes for the future and contentment with the
present.[23]

Modern scholars have often taken such praises and the imperial
cult itself as a purely formal gesture, "an instrument of rule, a
bond of imperial loyalty." Such, indeed, it was in some ways, but
there was a deeper connotation to the cult of the Roman sover-
eigns, which after all began and flourished by the desires of the
subjects, not the rulers; "the imperial cult to some extent succeeded in mystifying political reality."[24]

At Rome too Augustus eventually became a revered symbol. In
his early days he had felt the anger of the populace, which once
sought to stone him when the naval blockade by Sextus Pompey
produced a food shortage; but after Actium food and games became far more secure. Yet Augustus ran into the old Republican
contradiction: the very people who were to be bought by largesses
of money and food were yet the sovereign font of power in the
Roman constitution. The citizen body might have been a rabble
in the eyes of Augustus and his associates, but it had to be kept
up to proper standards of religion, dress, and customs. Athletes
and actors were allowed greater privileges than ever before—for
Augustus really enjoyed the popular entertainments which he
gave in profusion—but overly presumptuous players were pun-
ished or exiled. On the one hand Augustus paraded his tribunician power on his coins as illustrating his care of the masses; on
the other hand he created an urban police which together with a
paramilitary fire brigade made Rome far more heavily supervised
than are modern capitals.

Still the people could shout, and they could whisper. In 22 B.C.
there rose a great popular demand that Augustus become dictator for life. The populace, indifferent to the subtleties of his compromise with the Senate, knew with simple insight that the "first
citizen" was really their lord and saw no reason for hiding their
knowledge. This outbreak Augustus could stop only by a public

appeal in which he tore open his toga and threatened to commit suicide. In A.D. 7, again, the people were overwrought because of frontier wars and a shortage of food, and a woman who practiced divination excited them yet more. To quiet the disorder Augustus made a public vow to celebrate a forthcoming festival magnificently "and proceeded to do anything that would make the crowd cheerful."[25]

His relations with the aristocracy were even more complicated, and full solution of the difficulties was never possible. He lived a simple life, much as did Leonardo de' Medici in Renaissance Florence, and avoided ostentation; his home was not yet the palace in which later emperors were to have a true court. He himself entertained often at dinner, and accepted almost all invitations to dinner with fellow aristocrats, such as Vedius Pollio; and he was personally accessible, though his bodyguard was immediately ready to kill one unfortunate supplicant who made him stumble. Until his last years he patiently sat in the Senate and genuinely tried to adjust his policies to aristocratic prejudices. Yet aristocrats as well as the masses knew that he was master and were more than ready to engage in adulation. The architect Vitruvius, who completed his treatise on architecture in 23 or 22 B.C., dedicated it with fulsome praise to Augustus, as did many other writers of the Augustan Age; Horace and Virgil genuinely and Ovid more hypocritically sang the praises of the restorer of peace.

Other aristocrats, however, could plot, though always in vain, or pass on the "chilling rumor which spreads from the Forum through the streets" about his relations with Livia, the sins of Julia, or less personal matters of state such as the course of events on the frontiers. One problem here was the fact that the regime had begun to wrap a veil of secrecy about its acts, and subordinates of the ruler tended to send their despatches solely to him, who relayed them to the Senate at his pleasure. Both Tacitus and Dio Cassius comment explicitly on the difficulties of writing history under this imperial veil; the pressures of flattery also endangered historical objectivity.[26] Worse from the point of view of imperial administration was the tendency of the Senate to abdicate even the measure of responsibility which Augustus still forced on it and the parallel reluctance of many aristocrats to serve the state in public office.

Here the poet Horace manifests a growing unease of sensitive men. Whereas Virgil remained true to the Augustan system until his death, the later poetry of Horace, especially the *Epistles,* suggests that he was brooding on "liberty," not in a political sense but in a more general social framework. Horace bitterly disliked the practical results of the Augustan world, which promoted a life of idle luxury among the aristocracy, and he retreated ever more within himself; in one epistle he even rejected the request of his patron Maecenas to return from his Sabine farm to Rome and broadened his rejection into a proclamation of independence—Maecenas, he asserted, did not make him rich merely to enforce obedience.[27]

Horace never directly addressed himself to the hidden possibility that the Augustan political system might generally mean slavery, but there were men who recognized this likelihood. The historian Asinius Pollio, for one, felt that liberty ended with the death of Brutus and Cassius at Philippi and that the conflict between Octavian and Antony had merely been to determine who would succeed the dead dictator Caesar. Under Nero the poet Lucan was to write his epic *Pharsalia* openly on the same theme, but it was never to be politically safe to assert publicly the ambiguity—Lucan's own life ended suddenly.

In sum Augustus steered the Empire along lines which it was to follow for centuries to come, both in its strengths and in its weaknesses; the latter often the consequence of artful compromise with the Republican past. When men of later generations looked back on Augustus, they tended to have mixed emotions. His memory among common folk stood high, and the great events of his reign were long commemorated by coins, calendars, and both public and court rites and festivals. Writers of aristocratic stamp from Seneca the Elder on accepted him as inevitable and necessary to stop the Roman revolution; yet these writers rejected almost unanimously his claim that he had restored the Republic. To them the Empire was an autocratic system, and Augustus was the first autocrat. If Augustus could have heard the voices of future generations as he lay on his deathbed and begged for the applause of the bystanders, his self-satisfaction might have been diminished.

Perhaps the best summation of the views held by his contemporaries is given by Francis Bacon's assessment of Henry VII Tudor, who was very similar to Augustus in that he calmed England after the protracted agony of the Wars of the Roses:

> As for the disposition of his subjects in general toward him, it stood thus with him; that of the three affections which naturally tie the hearts of the subjects to their sovereign,—love, fear, and reverence,—he had the last in height; the second in good measure; and so little of the first, as he was beholding to the other two.

In an earlier sketch Bacon described Henry as "a great observer of formality in all his proceedings, which notwithstanding was no impediment to the working of his will." No better description could be coined of the manner in which Augustus operated.[28]

Notes

1. Suetonius, *Augustus* 28; Aulus Gellius, *Attic Nights* 15. 7. 3 preserves a letter to his grandson in which Augustus hopes to be a good man in a state perfectly happy.
2. Appian, *Civil Wars* 5. 130.
3. *Il Principe* 4, quoted by G. P. Burton, *Journal of Roman Studies,* 67 (1977), p. 165, to whom I am indebted for the substance of the next few sentences.
4. Tacitus, *Histories* 1. 1; Dio Cassius, 53. 24. 6, on the execution of M. Egnatius Rufus in 19 B.C.
5. Seneca, *On Anger* 3. 23. 4–8; so too Seneca's father, *Controversies* 10. 522; Seneca, *On Benefits* 3. 27. 1.
6. Franz J. Biermann, "Augustus and the Pax Augusta," *Transactions of the American Philological Association,* 72 (1941), pp. xxviii–ix.
7. M. Corbier, "L'aerarium militare," *Armées et fiscalité dans le monde antique,* ed. A. Chastagnol et al. (Paris, 1977), pp. 197–234; as R. O. Fink, *Roman Military Records on Papyrus* (Cleveland, 1971), no. 77=P. Mich. 435, shows, soldiers who inherited only 100 drachmae from fellow soldiers paid the 5%.
8. Suetonius, *Augustus* 25.
9. *Res Gestae* 27.

10. Livy 4. 20, a chapter apparently added in light of the problem faced by Augustus; M. P. Charlesworth, *Cambridge Ancient History*, 10 (Cambridge, 1934), p. 125.

11. *Aeneid* 1. 278–82; in 6. 791–97 Augustus is expected to "extend his empire beyond the Indies."

12. Dio Cassius 56. 16; Suetonius, *Augustus* 23.

13. Suetonius, *Augustus* 41.

14. Ronald Syme, *The Roman Revolution* (Oxford, 1939), p. 454.

15. Vitruvius, *On Architecture* 1, Preface.

16. Suetonius, *Augustus* 31.

17. Suetonius, *Augustus* 98.

18. A. Ferrill, *Latomus*, 168 (1980), p. 338; Syme, *Roman Revolution*, p. 454, puts it that he "was a singularly archaic type."

19. Propertius 2. 7. 13–14.

20. Fronto, *To His Friends* 1.3 (Haines 1, p. 280); in *To Verus* 2. 7 (Haines 2, p. 154) Fronto asserts that affection in the family was "practically non-existent" at least among aristocrats. H. Dessau, *Inscriptiones Latinae Selectae* [hereafter Dessau], 8393 ("laudatio Turiae," edited and translated into French by M. Durry [Paris, 1950]).

21. Propertius 2. 6. 25–26, blunter than Horace, *Odes* 3. 6. 46–48.

22. Dio Cassius 54. 23; Pliny, *Natural History* 9. 77.

23. *Ancient Greek Inscriptions in the British Museum* 4. 1, ed. G. Hirschfeld (Oxford, 1893), no. 894; the translation in part by David Magie, *Roman Rule in Asia Minor*, 1 (Princeton, 1950), p. 490.

24. J. P. V. D. Balsdon, *Romans and Aliens* (London, 1979), p. 257; S. R. F. Price, *Journal of Roman Studies*, 80 (1980), p. 43.

25. Dio Cassius 55. 31. 3.

26. Horace, *Satires* 2. 6. 50; Tacitus, *Annals* 1. 1; Dio Cassius 53. 19; also Seneca, *To Marcia* 4. 3.

27. *Epistle* 1. 7.

28. Francis Bacon, *History of the Reign of King Henry VII* (*The Works of Francis Bacon*, ed. James Spedding et al., 11 [Boston, 1860]), pp. 362, 38–39.

CHAPTER II

The Imperial Succession

Once consolidated the Empire was ruled by a famous series of Roman Caesars, for whom we have a wealth of gossipy detail in the biographies of Suetonius and the Augustan History as well as other literary works of the Early Empire. So Nero appears, a lyre-playing ruler in command performances, where the doors were guarded so that no one could leave in boredom; legend has it that once a pregnant woman came to her time at such a recital but had to give birth in the hall—a rather unlikely tale in view of the hubbub which might have occurred. The obscure general Vespasian did make the mistake of falling asleep at one Neronian session but survived to become master himself. Bluff and direct, the first emperor not descended from the Roman aristocratic class, Vespasian put a tax on public urinals; when his son Titus objected in disdain, Vespasian picked up some coins and said, "They don't smell, do they?"[1] Or there is Hadrian, always curious and unstable, climbing Etna to see the sunrise or founding a whole new city in Egypt to memorialize his dead favorite Antinous.

The humorous or horrible incidents of imperial whim could be multiplied indefinitely; from the Renaissance onward they have provided illustrations and allusions in court life and modern literature. Undoubtedly the character and interests of a ruler could have pronounced effects both in Rome and in the provinces; among the most significant down to A.D. 211 were Claudius, Vespasian, Hadrian, and Septimius Severus (see Table of Emperors). Yet just as American history is not simply a series of presidencies so too there was continuity in the development of the Empire which was independent of personality. General analysis of the position of the emperor is made easier by the fact that there was no fundamental change in the forces governing succession, survival, and the imperial position proper. Only in such externals as the elaboration of pomp and administrative machinery was there real expansion and alteration. The continuity of the Principate reign after reign, however, eventually led all important groups in the Empire to accept the presence of a ruler as a vital requirement for the well-being of the subjects and thus an important element in the survival of the realm.

Succession

Let us begin by considering the problems of succession in themselves. In legal theory, as already noted, the Empire did not experience true hereditary rule. It had no crown nor even a throne in the literal sense, and little ceremony of court at the outset; the powers of state came from the people and reverted to the people on the death of any one holder. Yet Augustus intended a hereditary succession, and his contemporaries as well as the next two generations accepted this principle without serious objection; an imperial virtue, celebrated on coins, was an emperor's foresight in arranging for transfer of power (*designatio*).[2] Such a pattern made it legally easier to pass on the ruler's personal estate or *patrimonium,* which was already extensive under Augustus and was enlarged by bequests and additions from the property of condemned political criminals. Although later rulers sometimes made gifts of land to favorites, mistresses, or wives, the *patrimonium* of the emperor tended to become ever larger as aristocrats were sent to the block.

Tiberius followed Augustus in A.D. 14 without difficulty; on Tiberius' death in A.D. 37 the young Gaius (nicknamed Caligula) became ruler and was hailed as "the new sun" after the last gloomy days of his great-uncle—an interesting illustration of an attitude toward royalty which recurred, for instance, in Elizabeth I of England as the Sun Queen and Louis XIV of France as the sun-god.[3] Gaius swiftly lost the favor of the people, of the Senate, and of his own administrators and so fell. When Gaius was murdered the Praetorian Guard ransacked the palace and found his uncle Claudius cowering behind a wall-hanging; over the objection of the Senate the praetorians made him ruler, and in return Claudius began the custom of rewarding the Guard by an accession donative. He in turn became victim to a dish of poisoned mushrooms prepared by his wife Agrippina, and her son Nero inherited power.

Like Gaius, Nero alienated one vital group after another; when Galba, governor in Spain, revolted, the Senate plucked up its courage and proclaimed Nero an outlaw. On his suicide no one of the Julio-Claudian clan qualified for the succession, and in any event the generals of the Empire had fallen into contest to see who should gain the imperial purple. In the civil wars of 68–69 Galba, Otho, and Vitellius held the throne briefly before Vespasian emerged the ultimate victor. A small faction in the Senate opposed his principle of hereditary succession through philosophic argument but in vain; Vespasian's two sons Titus and Domitian duly came into office. After the murder of Domitian an aged aristocrat Nerva was elevated as emperor, but threatening noises from the armies quickly led him to adopt the nearest competent general, Trajan. Across the second century physiological accident produced the series of "good emperors"—Trajan, Hadrian, Antoninus Pius—none of whom had sons; the last of the group, Marcus Aurelius, however, did, and Commodus duly became emperor, ruled badly, and was strangled on the last day of 192. The plotters had picked the distinguished Pertinax to succeed; but Pertinax quickly lost the support of the Guard by his parsimony and was killed. The throne was thus left open, and the decision as to its occupant was settled by new civil wars. Septimius Severus eventually won but felt it desirable to consolidate his legal position by securing posthumous adoption into the Antonine clan.

One requirement for formal succession, thus, was blood or fictive relationship to the preceding ruler, partly in order to make it legally easier to pass on the *patrimonium* but more because of natural human feelings. The other requirements were basically (1) a law or laws granting full legal powers to the new ruler; (2) acceptance by the Senate on behalf of the state and bestowal of *imperium* after a formal play (*recusatio*) in which the ruler professed his unworthiness and the Senate, thus ostensibly showing its free choice, forced him to accept the inevitable; (3) an expression of loyalty by the armies of the Empire through the taking of oaths, which were annually renewed on the ruler's day of accession (*dies imperii*), and more particularly the salutation by the Praetorian Guard on behalf of the armed forces. Rulers dated the beginning of their reign from the day of their grant of *imperium;* Vespasian more realistically chose the day when he was proclaimed emperor by the army in Alexandria and so had to have the date of his law put back half a year to justify his actions before he entered Rome.

The most important single succession was certainly the first, that of Tiberius, which consolidated the principle that Rome would continue to be ruled by a *princeps*. When the aged Augustus breathed his last in August of A.D. 14 Tiberius was already regent; the grant of all major legal powers had taken place two years earlier, and he lacked only some of Augustus' titles such as *pater patriae* and *imperator* (which he never assumed). On the death of his adopted father Tiberius sent despatches to the army and gave the watchword to the Praetorian Guard; at Rome, in Tacitus' words, "all—consuls, senators, and equestrians—plunged into servitude" by taking an oath of allegiance to Tiberius.[4]

Augustus' proconsular *imperium* had duly been extended for five- or ten-year periods several times by the Senate, a formality which Tiberius must have observed on occasion; but when it came time, after the funeral of Augustus, for him to execute the scenario listed in step 2 above, matters went far less well than at the hands of the urbane, patient Augustus. Tiberius, a weary man of 54, displayed a real reluctance to take up the burdens of state; at the meeting of the Senate where his *recusatio* was performed he eventually suggested that he accept only part of the responsibilities. A bold senator asked him "Which part?," and Tiberius had to admit that power was indivisible.

Although the armies had duly sworn their oaths of allegiance to the new *princeps,* Tiberius probably knew by the day of the Senate meeting that the Pannonian legions had revolted, as did also the armies of Germany. These revolts were not against the ruler *per se* but against harsh conditions of military service. They were, indeed, the most significant military upheavals in the Early Empire that were caused by the troops themselves rather than being the result of incitements and bribes by ambitious generals; probably they are the most telling examples of the slackness and inefficiency of Augustus' last years. Tiberius' son Drusus, sent to Pannonia, quickly restored order there; the popular young hero Germanicus, nephew of Tiberius, was already on the Rhine and in a bumbling fashion eventually redressed the situation among the German legions. So began a reign which was to go from bad to worse despite the serious efforts of Tiberius to administer conscientiously and to respect the authority of the Senate.

Apart from the "good emperors" most rulers after Tiberius came to power in less-secure fashion; there were, accordingly, psychological and ideological requirements to be met by each new *princeps* for him to gain the necessary charisma as guardian of imperial order and strength. Even Octavian in his earliest days had had to counter charges of effeminacy and cowardice by displaying personal valor in battle and siege and by emphasizing his masculinity in statues and portraits. So too each new ruler despatched statues (sometimes busts which could be inserted into the statue of a previous emperor) and painted representations to the provinces; as the orator Fronto wrote to his pupil Marcus Aurelius,

> You know how in all money-changers' bureaus, booths, bookstalls, eaves, porches, windows, anywhere and everywhere there are likenesses of you exposed to view, badly enough painted most of them to be sure, and modelled or carved in a plain, not to say sorry, style of art.[5]

The ancient world unfortunately lacked the technique of photography, which so easily reproduces the visages of modern rulers.

Probably the most interesting propaganda campaign for a new ruler came on the accession of Vespasian, who as victor in the bloody civil wars of 68–69 desperately needed psychological and spiritual justification. While in Alexandria he was asked to heal a blind man and a man with a withered hand; when he gave them his saliva they were immediately cured. He was hailed as the god Sarapis himself, and the miracles were widely publicized—one papyrus survives which records the acclamation of Vespasian by the people of Alexandria as Savior and Benefactor. There were also Jewish prophecies that a man from Judaea would rule the world; this was refashioned to fit Vespasian and his son Titus, in charge at the time of putting down the Jewish revolt! To gain western support Vespasian also engaged in a moderate rehabilitation of Galba, and had himself acclaimed *imperator* for military victories 20 times during his relatively brief reign (Augustus had only 21 such acclamations in his whole life).

Caesars might be praised by provincials for bringing peace to the Empire, but to consolidate their reputation in more important sectors military prowess also had to be paraded. One of the most extreme illustrations of this requirement is provided by the unexpected accession of the gangling, unwarlike Claudius, who seized on an ephemeral success of a general in Mauretania Tingitana to celebrate a victory in his first year (the area was already in revolt again the next year); the unfortunate conquest of Britain was launched partly to reenforce his reputation among the armies and generals.

If a ruler followed an unpopular or murdered *princeps,* his administration would promptly permit general public damnation of the predecessor as a despotic tyrant, and the ruler himself could stress a policy of peace, law, and restoration of liberty; this latter blessing for some reason continued to need periodic resuscitation on into the reign of the Gothic king Theodoric in the sixth century, "guardian of liberty and propagator of the Roman name," as an inscription puts it.[6] Accompanying this proclamation would come massive celebrations of the virtues of the new regime on the coinage—peace, felicity, serenity, and other noble claims chosen either by the ruler himself or by one of his aides. If, on the other hand, the new *princeps* came to power without friction, he sought to link himself to his predecessor by change of name and other actions and could make allusions in his coinage to past reigns; Trajan in particular issued a volume of coinage which repeated in silver Republican types and in gold celebrated all first-century rulers save Gaius, Nero, Otho, Vitellius, and Domitian. By this time continuity of administration was becoming more evident, and the aristocracy had become resigned; Tacitus could even say of Nerva that he conjoined two opposites previously incompatible, "the principate and liberty."[7] Succession for a time became almost automatic.

Survival

In view of the peculiarities of the political theory of the Empire the Caesars were in a fundamentally unstable position, for anyone could claim power who could suborn the people to give *him* the proper authority by law. The praetorian prefect Sejanus came very close to success in his endeavor to unseat Tiberius, who had eventually immured himself far from Rome on the island of Capri. On the other hand rulers could count on a natural tendency of human nature to accept a situation once it was stabilized. To make certain, however, it was desirable to remove possible contenders within or without the imperial family. On the accession of Tiberius the last grandson of Augustus, Agrippa Postumus, was immediately killed, though Tiberius insisted that the deed was not done on his initiative. Likewise in the reigns of Gaius, Nero, and Domitian relatives were pitilessly eliminated; Hadrian, who came to power through a rather dubious deathbed adoption by Trajan, promptly ordered the execution of four leading consulars who might be dangerous competitors.[8]

After gaining the throne emperors had to maintain harmonious relations with three groups or sources of power if they were to survive long. One, naturally, was their own entourage of advisers, administrators, and servants, extending as far as the Praetorian Guard of nine cohorts which Tiberius concentrated in a fortified camp on the edge of Rome; in regular rota its units guarded the palace, but the imperial bedchamber was protected by a corps of Germans through the Julio-Claudian period. Any ruler—specifically Gaius, Nero, Domitian, Commodus, and Pertinax—who lost the support of this staff was doomed, for the way to assassination lay open. Yet by and large the staff was not self-moving in abandoning a ruler; in such cases either the armies or the senatorial aristocracy, or both, had turned against the emperor.

On this level the role of the Praetorian Guard in making and unmaking emperors has often been much exaggerated. True, its loyalty was decisive; when Tiberius finally moved against Sejanus his agents were uncertain how far the Guard had been corrupted and used the urban cohorts of police instead to surround the decisive Senate meeting which condemned Sejanus. On his fall the Guard was duly rewarded by a donative, and wise rulers saw to it that bonuses were distributed at festivals and on other occasions. The churlish, miserly Galba did not make the customary payment—"I select my troops, I don't buy them"—and so his reign lasted only 91 days;[9] but it was a legionary, not a praetorian, who killed him. Only twice in the first two centuries did praetorians commit the fatal deed (Gaius and Pertinax); while the Guard had abandoned Nero, it remained loyal to Domitian and forced Nerva to execute the assassins of Domitian.

The emperors had also to retain the loyalty of the armies on the frontier. When major blocks of troops revolted against the shame of their lyre-playing emperor Nero his end was inevitable. One of his immediate successors, Vitellius, stressed "agreement of the armies" (*consensus exercituum*) on his coinage along with *concordia praetorianorum* and *fides exercituum;* the first of these slogans reappeared on the coins of Vespasian, Nerva, and later rulers.[10] On the whole, however, as we shall see when we examine the armed forces of the Empire in detail, they tended toward loyalty; provincial governors and army commanders could not easily move the troops against the central government. In war the emperors themselves very often came to the scene of action, save for Nero and Antoninus Pius. In Nero's case the result was that he had to execute Corbulo, the forceful general who restored the frontier in Asia Minor; and Domitian became so suspicious of Agricola, who went far toward conquering Scotland, that this general was forced into retirement. Vespasian was picked to put down the Jewish revolt in part because his ancestry was not noble; and all rulers watched their governors and generals carefully lest they become too popular or league together.

The third essential element was the senatorial aristocracy, which no longer governed but was vital to the ruler in providing personnel for his government and in determining the tone and judgment of Roman society. Here too we must take up developments more fully in a subsequent chapter, but the fate of Gaius, Nero, Domitian, and Commodus luridly illuminates the hidden power of the aristocracy, quite independent of the army. Far too often historians of the Roman Empire minimize this strength, but the emperors who survived paid as much attention to the attitudes of this group as had Augustus. If, as in the case of Vespasian's suppression of the philosophic opposition to hereditary rule, they had to stand against an aristocratic pressure they did so reluctantly and with great caution.

Two groups in the Roman world remain which might be thought to exert some weight in the survival of an emperor: the Roman populace itself and the mass of provincial subjects. The former could and did demonstrate in the streets or more often in the Colosseum and Circus Maximus, and at times the emperors would yield a favorite to their hostility; but never once in the Early Empire did the *populus Romanus* overthrow or even threaten the power of an emperor, who after all safeguarded their food supplies and provided entertainments as a rule with a lavish hand.

The provinces likewise were not an obviously active factor in the selection or retention of rulers. Once a provincial uprising—that of Vindex in Gaul—did set in motion a chain of events which led to the overthrow of Nero (and in the third century a revolt in Africa was to cause the fall of the emperor Maximinus); but even during the civil wars of 68–69 and 193–95 the provinces were essentially passive while the legions marched to and fro. Still, the emperors kept their finger on the pulse, or pulses, of the Roman world; the correspondence between Trajan and Pliny the Younger as governor of Bithynia concerns the most minute of detail, though this province, recently troubled, may not have been entirely typical. Under the same ruler the great orator Dio Chrysostom was virtually a press agent for the new regime in delivering speeches to the Greek East on the virtues of the ruler and the blessings of Roman order. In return the provincials swore oaths of allegiance at least under Gaius and some other emperors, set up honorary inscriptions and altars, and in public gatherings chanted the praises of their far-off master in set terms which eventually were codified in a manual by the grammarian Menander, who begins by warning that encomiums of an emperor were not to suggest that the present good qualities of the ruler could be increased, or that any part of his rule was debatable.[11]

The Imperial Position

Before we consider the position of the emperor in day-to-day life as administrator of the Empire and patron of culture we must return once more to a problem treated only briefly in the Augustan period. Was the Empire in essence a regime of law?

Any objective answer to this intricate and difficult question must cope with two serious sources of distortion, one ancient, the other modern. The literary works of the Early Empire are, to wit, almost entirely the product of aristocratic pens or written by authors who enjoyed aristocratic patronage; men of this stamp had no doubt the Empire was autocratic in root, for aristocrats no longer had the direct authority which they had wielded in the Republic—even though, as just argued, they did not become totally insignificant. As a recent scholar has dryly commented, "It is often maintained that history is the history of the ruling class. Roman imperial history is the version of the ex-ruling class."[12] Sometimes, as in Tacitus' *Annals* and *Histories,* the imperial system was depicted in a bitterly hostile light; at other times the concession was made that monarchy was inevitable and did favor peace or that the present ruler was better than his predecessor, but the point of view remained the same. Yet autocracy is not always *per se* illegal, despite Lord Acton's pronouncement that absolute power tends to corrupt.

Then again the imperial pretense that power came from the people by voluntary grant, whereas it was either seized or inherited, reminds some modern scholars uncomfortably of the theory and practice in contemporary Communist states. As Henry Kissinger majestically commented,

> No Communist state has solved the problem of regular succession. Every leader dies in office, or is replaced by couplike procedures. Honorific retirement is rare and nonexistent for the supreme leader. No Soviet leader's reputation, except Lenin's, has survived

his death. In every Communist state a leadership group seize power, grow old together, and are eventually replaced by successors whose ability to reach the pinnacle depends on their skill in masking their ambitions . . . they know that they will probably be denied by their successors the accolade of history, which is the incentive of most statesmen.

Beside Kissinger's last point a historian of the Roman Empire can place a comment by Dio Cassius, "No injunction can have any weight against the ingratitude or the might of one's successors."[13]

The Roman Empire, however, was not encumbered with the weight of Marxist-Leninist doctrine, nor was it the heir of Russian tsars; rather it emerged out of the Roman Republic and was very poorly equipped with political theory. If we turn and look at the emperors themselves, it quickly becomes apparent that they did not act like Republican consuls, elected in pairs for only one year and fettered by the Senate and by ancestral custom; in many ways their role resembles that of a provincial governor in the Republic, essentially absolute in his province and adulated by his subjects (at least in the Greek East). The summation of a Republican governor's position applies equally well to the Roman Caesars: "A Roman governor was either a wonderful success or a gigantic failure; and the opportunities of harm possessed by a vicious and incompetent administrator were beyond calculation."[14]

Emperors such as Nero and Domitian did become tyrannical; after all they had force at their disposal, and as a wise American historian of the earlier nineteenth century noted, "The might to govern must of necessity carry with it the right to govern; and in this sense,—and a very important sense it is too,—Might does actually make Right." But the fact that power could be held by despots does not mean that the imperial position was theoretically untrammeled. Too much can be made—and sometimes has been—of a terse pronouncement by the great jurist Ulpian, "the *princeps* is exempted from laws."[15] Since we lack the context we do not know whether the emperor was exempted from all laws or only limitations such as those applied to men with less than three children, or indeed whether the exemption was itself cast in the form of a law or merely reflected codification of custom. In practice, in any case, an emperor oculd not expect to issue any directive which he wished or to have every whim honored; precedents, often incorporated into the very structure of government, could sabotage a specific order, and in the long run a ruler did well to keep in mind the prejudices and opinions of the army and the senatorial aristocracy.

At the least, thus, there were conventions, rules, and actual laws in the Early Empire which controlled the lives of all but one man, and most commonly that individual found it safer and more prudent to appear as if they governed him too. In my judgment we can go further and properly conclude that most rulers sincerely believed and acted as if their powers were to be used responsibly for the benefit of the state and conceived, as Marcus Aurelius put it early in his *Meditations,* "the idea of a commonwealth based on equity and freedom of speech, and of a monarchy cherishing above all the liberty of the subject." In the second century, interestingly, there appeared the argument that the Roman Empire was the perfect democracy; when each class does what it best can do, "all will gain the true democracy and the freedom which does not fail." The complexity of the Augustan solution is, to conclude, well summed up in the remark, "If Imperial power was virtually unrestricted, it was also legitimate and based on the consent of the majority of senators, as well as that of other orders." On this level there was no evolution across the Early Empire, only incidental variation; a speaker in Tacitus' *Histories* put it neatly, "He prayed for good emperors, but took them as they came."[16]

In his daily life, the *princeps,* like any monarch, could work as much or as little as he chose, especially after an articulated central government began to emerge in the reforms of Claudius. Commodus, who spent his time largely in athletics, thus is not known to have issued any rescripts which extended the corpus of Roman law. Most emperors, however, appear to have been reasonably diligent even if, like Antoninus Pius, they could take simple vacations to help press grapes; apart from Hadrian's great processions no ruler after Augustus travelled extensively in the provinces in peacetime. Vespasian, for instance, rose before dawn and studied documents submitted by his secretaries, which he discussed with his "friends" (*amici*), a powerful group to which we shall return in Chapter IV. So too Septimius Severus was active before dawn, then took a walk in which he was informed of imperial events before hearing cases until noon. Thereafter he rode, visited the gymnasium and baths, had lunch and a nap, and once again took up duties of state until dinner. Marcus Aurelius, far too conscientious in a pettifogging way, even listened to litigants far into the night—after directing his serious Danubian wars by day—before wearily turning to write another section of repetitious, abrupt aphorisms in his *Meditations*— "Everything above and below is ever the same, and the result of the same things. How long then?"[17]

Fortunately for the emperors one of the trappings of autocracy, a true court life, evolved only slowly. Augustus lived a very simple life; even as late as Claudius the emperor could walk freely about the Palatine hill and casually drop in on a rhetorical performance. By the reign of Nero, who designed a huge palace, the Golden House, external pomp was growing; Domitian had constructed for himself an audience hall with soaring vault, one of the great steps in the evolution of Roman architecture. Antoninus Pius was in the eyes of his adopted son Marcus Aurelius "no connoisseur of the table, of the stuff and colour of his dress, of the beauty of his slaves"—a remark which suggests that other second-century emperors such as Hadrian were so concerned; by this time the morning levée of the ruler had become a regular ceremony, at which aristocrats and men of letters gathered to talk before being admitted to "salute Caesar." At the end of the second century imperial splendor had become extensive enough to cause one sophist to break down in his speech before Septimius Severus' court and bodyguard.[18]

The role of the ruler in administering justice, directing war, and supervising the imperial administration was of utmost significance in maintaining imperial unity, but these aspects may be reserved for later chapters. All Caesars had another important, demanding function, that of patron of culture. No emperor came close to equalling Augustus as an orator "with imperial fluency and spontaneity"; he even wrote tragedies in his youth though he jested his *Ajax* had slipped on a sponge (i.e., had been erased).[19] Yet his successors were educated in the classical tradition so that almost all, save perhaps Trajan, spoke both Greek and Latin; imperial rescripts in law as well as letters and other administrative documents reflect, despite official jargon, the varied temperament of each ruler and at times his own personal comment. Hadrian and Marcus Aurelius wrote extensively as emperors, but even the warrior Trajan had time to compose an account of his wars (from which one sentence survives in a grammatical quotation).

So the Caesars served as patrons of poets and other authors, whose works were collected in state libraries; gave public support and exemptions from taxes to professors of rhetoric and other subjects from the time of Vespasian; created literary competitions; and promoted the decoration of the capital with ever more lavish temples and other buildings. They graced public occasions with their presence, even at times for bizarre entertainments; Vespasian, though aged, was in the audience at the theater of Marcellus for the performance of a dog which appeared to die and then be reborn.[20]

Above all the rulers had to listen to speeches—complaints or praises by provincial delegations, orations of thanks for public office delivered in the Senate (though the one surviving example, Pliny's *Panegyric* before Trajan, is in its present form certainly much too long for complete recital), showy displays by visiting or local rhetoricians. Bored though they might be, the emperors had to attend; Antoninus Pius wrote once to Fronto in amazement, "What astonishes me . . . best of orators, is that . . . you can find anything to say that is new and worthy of your abilities."[21] For the Empire was held together not solely by the hobnailed boots of soldiers but also by the great weight of Greek and Latin rhetorical education which united the upper classes everywhere.

In a work designed to bend the young Nero toward virtue Seneca began with a spectacular portrayal of the absolute power of the ruler:

Have I [muses Nero] of all mortals found favour with Heaven and been chosen to serve on earth as vicar of the gods? I am the arbiter of life and death for the nations; it rests in my power what each man's lot and state shall be; by my lips Fortune proclaims what gift she would bestow on each human being; from my utterance peoples and cities gather reasons for rejoicing; without my favour and grace no part of the wide world can prosper; all those many thousands of swords which my peace restrains will be drawn at my nod; what nations shall be utterly destroyed, which banished, which shall receive the gift of liberty, which have it taken from them, what kings shall become slaves and whose heads shall be crowned with royal honour, what cities shall fall and which shall rise—this it is mine to decree.

With all things thus at my disposal, I have been moved neither by anger nor youthful impulse to unjust punishment, nor by the fool-hardiness and obstinacy of men which have often wrung patience from even the serenest souls, nor yet by that vainglory which employs terror for the display of might—a dread but all too common use of great and lordly power. With me the sword is hidden, nay, is sheathed; I am sparing to the utmost of even the meanest blood; no man fails to find favour at my hands though he lack all else but the name of man . . . Today, if the immortal gods should require a reckoning from me, I am ready to give full tale of the human race.[22]

Later Seneca put the imperial position more succinctly as that of a man nailed to a pinnacle, who could no more hide himself than can the sun. Each ruler and his family was subject to the most scurrilous of gossip and wall graffiti; Messalina, wife of Claudius, was for example said to have challenged a prostitute and won by servicing 25 men in 24 hours. Even more dangerous was the well-nigh unbelievable adulation proferred in public and the tendency of men to ape the current modes of the ruler; "nearly all of us," said Pliny the Younger, "live according to the standards of one man."[23]

What is most remarkable in the imperial position is not that some rulers yielded to the forces impelling them to autocracy but that most resisted the temptation. As we saw earlier, however, their very life depended upon keeping a balance and retaining good relations with the central administration, the aristocracy, and the armies. In the general success of the early *principes* one important, continuing force toward the survival of the Empire was consolidated. To return to Seneca,

> [The emperor] is the bond by which the commonwealth is united, the breath of life which these many thousands draw, who in their own strength would be only a burden to themselves and the prey of others if the great mind of the empire should be withdrawn . . . Such a calamity would be the destruction of the Roman peace, such a calamity will force the fortune of a mighty people to its downfall. Just so long will this people be free from that danger as it shall know how to submit to the rein; but if ever it shall tear away the rein, or shall not suffer it to be replaced if shaken loose by some mishap, then this unity and this fabric of mightiest empire will fly into many parts.[24]

Notes

1. Dio Cassius 65. 14 (hence the French word "vespasiennes").
2. M. P. Charlesworth, *Harvard Theological Review*, 29 (1936), pp 107–32.
3. *The Courts of Europe*, ed. A. G. Dickens (London, 1977), pp. 162 242.
4. Tacitus, *Annals* 1. 7.
5. Fronto, *To Marcus Caesar* 4. 12 (Haines, p. 206).
6. Dessau 827.
7. *Coins of the Roman Empire in the British Museum*, 3 (London 1936), p. xci; Tacitus, *Agricola* 3.
8. *Coins of the Roman Empire in the British Museum*, 2 (London 1930), p. 237, no. 5, shows Trajan and Hadrian holding hands with the legend ADOPTIO, a remarkable indication of the problems in Hadrian's accession.
9. Tacitus, *Histories* 1. 5; Dio Cassius 63. 3.
10. *Coins of the Roman Empire in the British Museum*, 1 (London 1923), pp. 385ff.; 2 (London, 1930), pp. 67ff.
11. *Menander Rhetor*, ed. D. A. Russell and N. G. Wilson (Oxford 1980).
12. B. Baldwin, *Ancient Society*, 3 (1972), p. 162.
13. Dio Cassius 59. 1; Henry Kissinger, *White House Years*, 1 (New York, 1979), p. 1139.

14. W. T. Arnold, *The Roman System of Provincial Administration* (3d ed.; Oxford, 1914), p. 55.

15. Richard Hildreth, *Theory of Politics* (New York, 1853), p. 20; *Digest* 1. 3. 31.

16. Marcus Aurelius, *Meditations* 1. 15; Dio Cassius 52. 14 (the concept of perfect democracy appears also in Philostratus, *Life of Apollonius* 5. 35, and Aelius Aristides, *On Rome* 60); P. Garnsey, *Social Status and Legal Privilege in the Roman Empire* (Oxford, 1970), p. 106; Tacitus, *Histories* 4. 8.

17. *Meditations* 6. 46.

18. Marcus Aurelius, *Meditations* 6. 16; Philostratus, *Lives of the Sophists* 614. Levée: Philostratus, *Life of Apollonius* 7. 31; Aulus Gellius, *Attic Nights* 4. 1, 19. 13, 20. 1.

19. Tacitus, *Annals* 13. 3, who sums up the oratorical abilities of rulers to his own day; only Nero and Domitian come off badly. *Ajax:* Macrobius, *Saturnalia* 2. 4.

20. Plutarch, *Moralia* 974a.

21. Fronto, *To Antoninus Pius* 2 (Haines 1, p. 126).

22. *On Clemency* 1. 1. 2–4.

23. So reports Pliny the Elder, *Natural History* 10. 172, who was alive at the time—though that does not guarantee its truth; Pliny, *Panegyric* 45. 5.

24. *On Clemency* 1. 4. 1–2.

CHAPTER III

The Roman Aristocracy

No ruler could by himself carry all the burdens of decisions and supervision of the imperial government. An obvious fact; the issue of import was where the emperor would turn to secure his advisers, his personal staff, and the governors, generals, and financial officials of the vast Empire. In the palace itself a growing number of imperial slaves and freedmen provided the mechanics of administration; establishment of policy was a more taxing matter, for which the monarch needed counsellors of wisdom and experience. From Augustus onward these advisers and the greater imperial officials were drawn from the Roman aristocracy, primarily its senatorial level but for some posts also the secondary equestrian class. As a Roman historian put it, "Major business demands major aides"; or to put the same problem in a different light, "What good thing could an ignorant or low-born person accomplish?"[1]

This was one of the most important compromises with the Roman past made by Augustus, and one which was to prove a source of continuing friction, from both sides, with respect to the relations of the aristocracy and the ruler. The ambivalent nature of the Empire as a regime of law shows here again and again in specific conflicts; the Caesars could neither govern without the aristocrats nor permit them true independence. Yet no later ruler sought to reverse the Augustan decision. Neither Gaius nor Nero, coupled by Pliny the Elder as "destroyers of the human race," engaged in anything like the wholesale murders of the young Octavian; the victims of Nero and other despotic masters were at times indeed primarily the bitter fruit of aristocratic factionalism.[2]

After all, the compromise did also have the positive virtue of enlisting an essential element of strength in upholding the unity of the Empire as it had earlier in the Republic. For the topmost level of Roman society had long been in existence, and to understand its characteristics under the Caesars we need to look briefly at its earlier history. The merger of old patrician and plebeian clans which had begun well before 300 B.C. was firmly consolidated by the Late Republic. At this time the senatorial aristocracy, as it is termed by modern historians, was distinct in dress, in seating at festivals, even in funerals where images of noble ancestors were paraded and a member of the clan pronounced a praise of the dead and his forebears. The term "liberty" which appears frequently in the literature of the Late Republic meant then primarily the right of aristocrats both to speak their own minds and to control the machinery of government.

Essentially the strength of this class depended upon its wealth. A recent study of imperial China makes a comment which applies equally well to Republican and imperial Rome: "Since wealth gave access to officialdom, and since official status protected and generated wealth . . . much modern scholarship has been devoted to clarifying whether wealth begot status or status wealth. But status and wealth were so intertwined and mutually supportive that question seems unanswerable."[3]

In Republican Rome riches had been gained largely by the spoils of war and profits of governorship, but then were mainly invested in land. Yet many landowners such as Cato the Censor in the second century or Crassus in the first century also supported companies of tax-farmers, lent money for overseas trade, and provided capital for freedmen to engage in local industry and trade. Cicero, who consciously voiced the aristocratic ethos, observed, "Trade, if it is on a small scale, is to be considered vulgar; but if wholesale and on a large scale, importing large quantities from all parts of the world and distributing to many without misrepresentation, it is not to be greatly disparaged. . . . But of all the occupations by which gain is secured, none is better than agriculture, none more profitable, none more delightful, none more becoming to a freeman."[4]

Caesar had bitterly offended his peers by parading open mastery; Augustus was far more shrewd by striking an outward compromise, in which the vehicle of the aristocracy—the Senate—was respected and its members could, at least in large part, be cajoled into serving the new order. Here, however, we must be explicit. No one today takes seriously Mommsen's theory that the Empire was a dyarchy in which Senate and emperors were equal; but while some historians consider the Empire an autocracy others suggest that one oligarchy was replaced by another: "in all ages, whatever the form and name of government . . . an oligarchy lurks behind the facade; and Roman history, Republican or Imperial, is the history of the governing class."[5] This view had led scholars to hunt for camarillas and hidden factions in the imperial court, whose contentions shaped the policy of the Empire. The search has produced little fruit, for we cannot see far into the secret councils of state; one may suspect that on occasion there was heated disagreement, but that the monarch in the end normally made the decisions. Even though the function of this chapter is to explore the nature of an important ingredient in the imperial structure, we must not thereby forget the role of the emperor, who was by Domitian's day more and more no longer *princeps* but lord (*dominus*).

Aristocracies of all ages do not stand in good repute these days with historians. They offend those of egalitarian instincts; their exploitive nature irks those of Marxist leanings; some modern examples have retained their social prominence without assuming the political responsibilities which theoretically justify their existence. Let us seek to cast off these blinkers and look more objectively first at the Senate as a corporate body, then the senatorial aristocracy, and finally the equestrian class.

The Senate and the Emperors

Augustus winnowed the Senate three times, both to shrink its numbers down to about 600 from the swollen 1000 produced by the favors of Antony and others and also to enhance its stability and dignity. We have already seen him appearing before it in January 27 B.C. to proclaim the restoration of constitutional government; thereafter he paid it deference and patiently sought its advice and judgment. On at least one occasion he did not care for that counsel and departed in anger; but on the whole he was tactful—and the senators both remembered his earlier ruthlessness and accepted with relief the cessation of internal disorder.

Tiberius was far less successful. Though the pressure of inevitability had forced him to accept the "slavery" of the imperial position he tried earnestly to make the Senate a real partner. Election of magistrates was transferred to the Senate, which thereby became a co-opting body entirely independent of the people; Tiberius lifted the veil of secrecy over imperial administration to a considerable degree; a yearly oath of allegiance to his acts by the Senate, which was later customary, he rejected; and he fostered freedom of debate in the Senate House to an extent which the historian Tacitus could not comprehend.

Tiberius perhaps brought down on himself the crisis of his later years by failing to note how far the hands of the clock had already moved. On the one hand the imperial household and central government were accustomed to look only to the ruler; on the other the affairs of the Empire could not again be subjected in every detail to the wrangling delays and personal factionalism of the Senate. The aristocracy, still split by family quarrels and rampant individualism, had, now that its responsibility was diminished, even less political cohesion than in the Late Republic. Repeatedly the Senate refused to take the initiative or even to make decisions, despite the warning of Tiberius that "every increase in prerogative was a weakening of the law." Rather it preferred to flatter and fawn at least in public; according to tradition Tiberius summed up the adulation in his bitter cry, "O men ready for slavery!"[6]

With Gaius the Senate experienced that slavery, and men's eyes were opened, if only briefly, to the frightful consequences of pushing the ruler toward open absolutism. When he was murdered in A.D. 41, no successor immediately appeared, and the following 24 hours witnessed a genuine effort by some groups to restore the Republic. The consuls immediately convened the Senate on the Capitol and gave the watchword *libertas* to the urban cohorts, but the Senate spent its precious moments of liberty in debating whether to reinstitute the Republic or to elect a new *princeps*. On the latter question old rivalries sprang to the fore; worst of all the Senate failed to gain support either from the people, who feared the greediness of the senators, or from the Praetorian Guard, which found and elevated Claudius to the throne. Throughout the following day the senators drifted to the praetorian camp to make their individual peace with the new emperor. By its evening Claudius was in the palace, and the next day he received the formal plaudits of the Senate. On the suicide of Nero 27 years later no one seriously raised the battle cry of the Republic.

The reign of Claudius prefigured in many respects the eventual solution of the relations between the ruler and the Senate. Claudius treated the Senate with outward consideration and endeavored to enforce attendance at its meetings. In one speech, preserved on papyrus, he sounds a note familiar alike under Tiberius and Trajan, for he recalls the slothful senators to a sober execution of their duty:

> If these proposals are approved by you, show your assent at once plainly and sincerely. If, however, you do not approve them then find some other remedies . . . It is extremely unfitting, Conscript Fathers, to the high dignity of this order that at this meeting one man only, the consul designate, should make a speech (and that copied exactly from the proposal of the consuls), while the rest utter one word only, "Agreed," and then after leaving the House remark "There, we've given our opinion.[7]

Whereupon, one suspects, the senators thanked Claudius for his encouragement to freedom of speech and then voted unanimously as they felt he desired; one senatorial decree of the reign asserted, "In nothing is it lawful to oppose the ruler."[8] In reality Claudius wielded a firm mastery over the Senate. Soldiers were forbidden to have social relationships with senators. The ruler reemphasized the Augustan controls of senatorial travel outside Italy. Equestrians were used in lesser provincial commands and other posts to an unprecedented degree; the central administration received its first regularization, as we shall see in the next chapter; even in Italy the emperor encroached on senatorial functions.

By the reign of Trajan the Senate outwardly was a sounding board or cheering section for imperial decisions. In thanks for his consulship Pliny the Younger delivered a massive *Panegyric* before Trajan in A.D. 100; soberly though it was meant we must blink when we read that the ruler ordered the Senate to be free and that "he will know when we use the freedom he gave that we are being obedient to him," or again that the Senate ordered its acclamations of Trajan to be engraved in bronze. The later historian Dio Cassius, active from Commodus onward for a generation, bitterly comments on the necessity of these praises which were chanted in unison.[9]

Although the Senate as a corporate body eventually became subservient, that is not quite all the story. Even in totalitarian states there is a need for congresses or assemblies, useful in giving honor to local dignitaries, in conveying programs and even problems of the central government back home, and in presenting a quiet opportunity for the masters to assess the views of the leading classes. Long after the Roman Senate had come fully to realize that it had neither ultimate authority nor responsibility one member arose in a debate over the costs of gladiatorial games in 177, began his remarks "although many think that on all matters referred to us by the Emperor we should give a single brief *sententia*," and went on to discuss the problem in detail.[10] Many senators had wide-ranging experience; the Senate, moreover, remained a continuing body while emperors might change, at times rather suddenly. Its function of counsel, in sum, remained important.

In this respect a change in the composition of the Senate took place which has often been measured statistically (as far as we can trust our somewhat accidental evidence). In the reign of Augustus 98 per cent of the senators were of Italian origin; only five senators may have derived from the provinces. In succeeding reigns this proportion sank, first slowly and then more rapidly. Under Trajan 55 per cent were Italian; among the provincial contingent itself 26 per cent were Gauls, 26 per cent Spaniards, 7 per cent Africans, and 41 per cent men from the Greek East. By Septimius Severus less than half of the Senate was of Italian stock. The Senate, thus "recruited from men of distinction in every province," came more and more to represent the Empire as a whole, and in that shift reflected the tighter unity achieved by the emperors and their administrations.[11]

Nevertheless the Senate remained "Roman" in important respects. Italians continued to be senators in a ratio disproportionate to the population of the peninsula, and those whose native language was Greek had to know Latin if they were to serve as officials and participate in senatorial sessions. Indeed many provincial senators may have come from ultimately Italian stock—55 of 69 known senators from Asia Minor down to Commodus were native of Roman colonies or cities where there were large Italian elements.[12]

Save for unfortunate exceptions the emperors from Augustus through Septimius Severus paid outward respect to the Senate; often this respect was embodied in a formal oath not to execute senators without a trial before their peers—though the oath was not always observed in practice. Amelioration of relations between the ruler and the Senate was facilitated by a delicate semantic shift in the term "liberty," which came to mean not senatorial license to govern but rather purely personal private freedom, safeguarded by the ruler's concern for social justice. And in final assessment it must never be forgotten that if the Senate became at least in part ornamental the underlying senatorial aristocracy remained truly powerful. No ruler who lost the support of this class, except to some degree Tiberius in his last years, survived to experience a natural death.

The Emperors and the Senatorial Aristocracy

The senatorial aristocracy had become a hereditary institution by the Late Republic; the main reforms of Augustus were to increase its property qualification and to grant only sons of senators the right to wear the "wide purple stripe" (*latus clavus*), though they officially remained equestrians until elected as quaestors.[13] Really firm public distinction between the two ranks of Roman aristocracy came in the reign of Claudius, but from Augustus onward would-be senators had to gain at least tacit assent of the emperor to enter public office and so perpetuate the glories of their clans. The Empire thus was "a hierarchic society of social climbers," an escalator onto which able men might step and rise; Augustus himself had shown the way by admitting many leaders of the Italian towns into the equestrian and senatorial orders.[14] Still, imperial choices were significantly limited by family pressures and the recommendations of those who were powerful in any one era.

Almost all men who desired a public career (*cursus*) served in their late teens in one of 20 posts (*vigintivirate*) controlling the streets of Rome, the mint, and other specialized functions. Thereafter an essentially civilian *cursus* led through the elected positions of quaestor (at about the age of 25), which brought membership in the Senate, aedile or tribune, and praetor at about 30; then might come the post of deputy of a governor for judicial business, the consulship, proconsulship of Asia or Africa, and perhaps at the peak of a successful *cursus* appointment by the emperor as prefect of the city, or governor of Rome. Men of this stamp were expected to spend a year or so in the army as a military tribune, but otherwise did not directly come under the ruler's authority. Elections, true, were influenced by the monarch's preference; 4 of the 10 praetors were directly nominated by him, and the consulship was very firmly controlled by imperial wishes.

Aspirants for fame or fortune, however, virtually had to enter the emperor's service; Tacitus sums up the crowning aspects of the public life of his father-in-law Agricola, "He had attained the ornaments of a triumph and the consulship; could Fate vouchsafe him more?"[15] More practically wars still brought booty, and the perquisites of governors were not inconsiderable. A young man could go on from the *vigintivirate* to old Republican magistracies but also serve the ruler directly as a military tribune for a more extended period, *legatus legionis* (a commander of a legion), a financial official, and governor of one or more imperial provinces in succession. Pertinax, emperor briefly in 193, had had, for example, a very unusual career. Son of a freedman, he had been a teacher for a while, then at the age of 34 asked his senatorial patron to secure him a legionary centurionate. Instead he was made prefect of a cohort in Syria, which placed him on the equestrian level. Thereafter he held a series of financial and military posts, in the latter of which he proved to be a competent general, able to cope with the growing threats of the late second century. So he was given membership in the Senate (*adlectio*) as an ex-praetor and became consul and prefect of the city before being chosen emperor.

From the point of view of the Caesars it was not altogether easy to get the senatorial aristocracy to bear its proper burdens of public life. Senatorial families died out, produced inadequate scions, or lost the wealth necessary to maintain their position (a minimum of one million sesterces from Augustus on). Any aris-tocracy, ancient or modern, fails to reproduce itself in time; the exact extent to which the phenomenon occurred in the Empire is difficult to measure. Apart from references by the historians we must rely for evidence on honorary or funeral inscriptions, which certainly give an incomplete picture, but it may be kept in mind that three successive emperors in the second century failed to produce sons. Moreover there could well have been families which simply ceased to pursue senatorial careers or others not of the first rank which only rarely provided an imperial adminis-trator. Augustus had to create new patrician clans to occupy cer-tain priesthoods, and already by the reign of Vespasian it was necessary to elevate additional families to this formal position. A speaker in the reign of Nero could assert that "most equestrians, many senators are descended from former slaves," and only eight families known to have existed in the Republic can still be found in the early third century after Christ.[16]

Even if we do not fully credit the contemporary picture of aris-tocratic vice in the Julio-Claudian era—Romans always had a strong puritanical streak about both sinning and detesting sin—it must have existed to some degree; rulers of the period more-over struck down a fair number of dangerous or displeasing aris-tocrats. From Vespasian on, we are informed, the upper classes lived in more sober fashion; but a recent historian has estimated that half the aristocracy in the second century consisted of "new men"—Pertinax can serve as one example.[17] The broadening of the Senate proper from an almost completely Italian group to an

Empire-wide selection may well have been a necessity as well as a desirable process.

The aristocracy also inherited from the past a desire for "dignified leisure"—*cum dignitate otium,* as Cicero had put it.[18] Politically retirement might well have had advantages in despotic reigns, though men learned under Nero that even outward neutrality was not permitted; as Dio Chrysostom ironically commented, no one dared to contradict Nero in anything—if he ordered someone to fly, the man promised to do so. Seneca after having been active in public affairs sought leave "from the Senate and the bar and all affairs of state, that he may retire to nobler affairs," though he went on to assert that a sincere and upright man would be grateful to those who did serve the state and allowed him his own peace of mind.[19]

There was, however, a far more fundamental reason why aristocrats might prefer *otium,* which did not in reality connote complete idleness. Their primary function and activity after all was the supervision and maintenance of their wealth. This was based above all on landed estates, though Roman aristocrats also drew important revenues from city property, loans, and financial support of freedmen in commerce and industry. Even the devoted public servant Pliny the Younger once asked a vacation from his post as director of the treasury to deal with his estates, and his letters return frequently to landed matters. His holdings appear to have been entirely in Italy, but other aristocrats had provincial farmlands especially in Africa, Sicily, and Gallia Narbonensis; at one point six men are said to have owned half of the Roman province of Africa (modern Tunisia).[20] In return senators of non-Italian origins, whose estates were presumably in their native provinces, had to place one third of their wealth in Italian land down to Marcus Aurelius and thereafter one fourth.

We cannot measure aristocratic wealth in any quantitative way. For Pliny the Younger there is enough information to support an estimate that he must have had over twice the capital of 8 million sesterces deemed necessary for senatorial life; one aristocrat is reported to have been worth 400 million sesterces. This figure is also assigned to the imperial freedman Narcissus under

Nero. For comparison Pompey, after his eastern conquests, may have attained a figure of 700 million sesterces; his contemporary Crassus is described as holding 200 million sesterces in land alone.[21] Income from rural estates devoted to grain seems to have run about 5 to 6 per cent, but was far less risky than overseas commerce. A recent argument that the emperors deliberately kept the public tax burden low so that the aristocrats, both Roman and local, could siphon off the profits of imperial prosperity is questionable; but certainly the aristocracy much enhanced its economic strength during the Early Empire.[22]

This aspect of the senatorial aristocracy was truly fundamental and must be kept in mind as we follow the vicissitudes of the Roman State through the troubled third century into the Later Empire. Men like both Plinys might serve the ruler, for the Republican tradition that the aristocracy should engage in public activity did not totally disappear, though men of the truly great clans were less likely to do so than middling aristocrats such as the Plinys. Under Hadrian one aristocrat actually declined a military command, but the deliberate mention of the fact quietly suggests that refusal may not have been easy or always safe.[23] Even so aristocrats did not often serve continuously; the career of Pertinax, outlined above, was at the time unusual in its concentration in public offices but presaged the rise of more professional generals and administrators. In the Early Empire itself recent estimates suggest that about half of the senators in any one reign were able or willing to take up imperial posts.[24]

The Equestrian Class

In considering the Roman aristocracy we are dealing with a minute fraction of the population of the Empire. The senatorial level was perhaps as low as 2/1000 of 1 per cent; the equestrian class, though far larger, was probably less than 1/10 of 1 per cent.[25] Equestrians had to have at least 400,000 sesterces in wealth; possibly there continued to be a register of those who were granted "the public horse"—a survival from the Early Republican provision of a horse to the cavalry—but on the whole accession to this class, permitted a narrow stripe of purple on togas and a gold ring, seems to have been relatively free. The position of an equestrian was not inheritable nor did it carry nobility for three generations, as did membership in the Senate.

Socially the equestrians fully shared the values and attitudes of senators. Ovid was an equestrian; we are incidentally informed that it was equestrians who led the opposition to Augustus' social legislation. Politically and economically, however, the equestrians had been marked off as distinct since the Gracchan reforms of the later second century B.C. They too held land as a base for wealth, but they also operated openly as tax-farmers, financiers, and money-lenders, and in general as "men of affairs." Seneca's brother Mela deliberately remained an equestrian so as to gain greater chances for wealth by "handling the emperor's business."[26]

Augustus broke fresh ground by employing equestrians in numbers as a counterbalance to the senatorial aristocracy. One route of equestrian advance was military and led through the post of military tribune, commander of an auxiliary unit, and then higher offices rising to command of the Praetorian Guard; non-equestrians originating in local upper classes could also take the rank of a legionary centurion at the age of about 30 and then become commander of an auxiliary unit. The other route usually also required first military service, then entry into financial positions as procurators of various types or, from Hadrian on, occupation of secretaryships in the central administration. Able equestrians also governed minor provinces such as Noricum and Judaea, but could hold far more important and sensitive posts. From Augustus on the governors of Egypt and commanders of its legionary garrisons were equestrians, so too after Claudius the commanders of the fleets based at Misenum and Ravenna, the largest military forces in Italy.

In a class-conscious world men from the second rung of imperial aristocracy were not likely to be able to woo armies into revolt, though Sejanus plotted almost with success to overthrow Tiberius. In the first two centuries of the Empire no equestrian became emperor (though Pertinax had passed through this level before being made a senator).

Together the senatorial and equestrian classes helped to bind together the very diverse territories under Roman rule by serving as governors, administrators, and generals who shared a common aristocratic stamp. This was a self-assured group which might yield deference in public demonstrations of loyalty but nonetheless had an independent position on its own estates; taken *en bloc* the aristocrats directly controlled a commanding proportion of the tangible wealth of the Empire. They also occupied a decisive role as patrons of that pattern of Greco-Roman culture which, as I stressed at the conclusion of Chapter II, was an equally vital cementing force. From Augustus on they essentially accepted the monarchs as masters; in return they gained outward dignity and increased distinction from commoners both in practice and in law. By the time of Hadrian senators bore the title of *vir clarissimus;* equestrians, that of *vir egregius.* There had been aristocrats before the Caesars began to rule Rome; there were still aristocrats when the last emperor in the west was deposed.

Notes

1. Velleius Paterculus 2. 127. 2; Dio Cassius 52. 8.
2. Pliny, *Natural History* 7. 45.
3. Charles O. Hucker, *China's Imperial Past* (Stanford, 1975), p. 339.
4. *On Offices* 1. 151.
5. Syme, *Roman Revolution,* p. 7.
6. Tacitus, *Annals* 3. 69. 6 and 3. 65. 3.
7. *Berliner Griechische Urkunden* 611; trans. by Charlesworth, *Cambridge Ancient History,* 10, pp. 697–98.
8. Pliny, *Letters* 8. 6. 10.
9. Pliny, *Panegyric* 67. 2, 78. 3; Dio Cassius 73. 20, 77. 6.
10. J. H. Oliver and R. E. A. Palmer, *Hesperia,* 24 (1955), p. 320.
11. Tacitus, *Histories* 1. 84; R. Etienne, *Les Empereurs romains d'Espagne* (Paris, 1965), p. 57.
12. C. Habicht, *Istanbuler Mitteilungen,* 9–10 (1959–60), pp. 121–23.
13. A. Ferrill, "The Senatorial Aristocracy in the Early Roman Empire," a paper delivered at the 1981 meetings of the Association of Ancient Historians.
14. A happy phrase of C. V. Wedgwood, *The King's Peace 1637–41* (New York, 1955), p. 433.

15. Tacitus, *Agricola* 44.
16. Tacitus, *Annals* 13. 27; A. Barbieri, *L'Albo senatorio da Settimio Severo a Carino (193–284 d. Chr.)*, (Rome, 1952), pp. 474–79.
17. Jones, *Later Roman Empire,* p. 5.
18. *pro Sestio* 98.
19. Dio Chrysostom 21. 6–10; Seneca, *Epistles* 73.
20. Pliny, *Natural History* 18. 35.
21. R. Duncan-Jones, *The Economy of the Roman Empire* (Cambridge, 1974), pp. 17ff.; Pliny, *Natural History* 33. 134; A. Ferrill, "The Wealth of Crassus and the Origins of the 'First Triumvirate,'" *Ancient World,* 1 (1978), pp. 169–77; I. Shatzman, *Senatorial Wealth and Roman Politics* (Brussels, 1975).
22. K. Hopkins, *Journal of Roman Studies,* 71 (1980), pp. 120–22.
23. Dessau 1071.
24. G. Alföldy, *Bonner Jahrbücher,* 169 (1969), p. 238, and W. Eck, *Aufstieg und Niedergang der römischen Welt* [hereafter ANRW], 2. 1 (Berlin, 1974), pp. 158–228, agree as against E. Birley, *Proceedings of the British Academy,* 39 (1953), pp. 197–214, who argues that less than half served.
25. Ramsay MacMullen, *Roman Social Relations 50 B.C. to A.D. 284* (New Haven, 1974), p. 88.
26. Tacitus, *Annals* 16. 17.

CHAPTER IV

Governing the Empire

The Roman Empire was a vast realm, one which embraced, moreover, peoples and cities on more diverse cultural and economic levels than is true even of Russia or China today. These variations will be approached more specifically in the next chapter; the problem to be faced here is the machinery by which the Empire was held together. Even if we omit much of the detail, our examination must be largely factual, at points statistical; but on its base rest important conclusions with respect to the survival of the Empire. First must come the manner in which imperial policy was set, then the structure which executed that policy, the costs thereof, and finally the vital matter of the provision of justice. The stinging query of Saint Augustine, "Justice being taken away, then, what are kingdoms but great robberies?" challenges every state in the course of history.[1]

Determination of Policy

For the machinery of government there is a considerable body of evidence in epigraphical, papyrological, and legal sources; for the formulation of policy we have much less. In practice there was, as already noted, a veil of secrecy according to Dio Cassius; when the executioners of Agrippa Postumus were directed by Tiberius to report to the Senate his advisor Sallustius vehemently opposed this exposure of *arcana imperii*. A daily gazette, the *acta,* was officially published in Rome, but this concerned religious prodigies, divorces, and minor matters as much as issues of state.

In the reign of Tiberius the ruler still actively took counsel with the Senate on revenues and taxes, letters to client kings, public works such as keeping the Tiber in its banks, discontent of the provincials, and a wide variety of other problems; his successors went through the formality of providing information and to some degree discussing matters in sessions of the Senate. Nero, for example, was dissuaded by the Senate in A.D. 58 from abolishing certain types of taxes. Active analysis and decisions on imperial policy, however, more and more were carried out by the emperor together with a small, select group of advisers. Usually these were aristocrats, but not always; Claudius reduced noble influence by relying on freedmen and could not escape the pressures of his wives; Vitellius and others also were much under the thumb of favorites; Commodus hearkened to a large extent to his concubine Marcia.

All rulers, nonetheless, had formal "friends" or *amici,* who often were taken over from a predecessor; Nerva thus retained Domitian's *amici* despite the violent change of power in 96. Titus was reported to have chosen his advisers "so as to prove indispensable to his successor as well, and the foremost servants of sovereign and state." Herein lay one source of continuing policy and a font of wisdom which the ruler could tap. The power of these "friends" was respected according to Epictetus,[2] and by the second century the institution had been formalized to some degree as a *consilium.* From Hadrian onward prominent jurists normally formed part of this council to assist the emperor in legal decisions; military experts can be detected as active advisers in the reigns of Antoninus Pius and Marcus Aurelius; for other ranges of problems men with special skills could be called into meetings of the council, as the letters of Pliny the Younger and a terse papyrus report of a session under Septimius Severus illustrate.

The *consilium* worked hard and certainly had some independence of judgment; Hadrian yielded his intention of abandoning the new conquest of Dacia on its advice, though Fronto, who much disliked this ruler, sneered—after Hadrian's death—that the emperor and his *amici* could not manage the armies.[3] Very probably cabals and factions emerged from time to time; but to repeat a view expressed in the previous chapter this does not force us to conclude that the Empire was in essence an oligarchy. By the second century the organs and principles of government had evolved so far that an individual ruler was less likely to institute wide-ranging reforms, such as those of Claudius; continuity in legislation is now quite evident. Still, the emperor was the master of the legions, and he had the responsibility for major decision.

His shoulders accordingly needed to be very broad. A recent extensive analysis of the emperor's role portrays him as largely passive, reacting to complaints and petitions from provincial assemblies, cities, and other bodies and individuals rather than launching out on new lines of public policy.[4] To some extent this picture is true; central governments must spend much of their energies in coping with issues brought up from lower levels. Yet it is not the complete story. The ruler, we are told again and again, kept his eye on imperial finances. He made or approved a wide range of military appointments; when the Empire fell into war with Parthia in the time of Marcus Aurelius a number of transfers or promotions followed in a deliberate chain. The letters between Trajan and Pliny as governor of Bithynia reveal the detail on which the central authority was consulted; and as has often been stressed even rulers accounted "bad" in Rome such as Tiberius and Domitian appear to have been efficient in supervising provincial administrators. When a new monarch took power, the line of propaganda as to public policy often shifted noticeably on the coinage of the realm. The Empire, in sum, did not simply drift, even though its masters did not consciously seek to direct economic and social change, which occurred slowly in an almost static system.

Machinery of Government

It is more proper to speak of the machinery or apparatus of government in the Early Empire than to employ the term "bureaucracy." There was a tendency to formalize the structure of the central offices and their provincial extensions and to develop rules of procedure. Two complaints against bureaucracy through the ages were levied against the imperial government: outcries by the subjects against official extortion and complaints by the rulers that "the evil-doing of men" prevented their orders from being carried out.[5] Yet down to 211 the organs of administration had not yet been systematized coherently. The Republican inheritance had been a hodgepodge of governmental institutions created *ad hoc* which had, in truth, been quite inadequate. From Augustus onward supervision of operations and personnel was more deliberate and careful, but the slowness of ancient communications still necessarily required considerable devolution of minor decisions to local units of government. In the second century only about 150 senatorial and equestrian officials were sent to the Roman provinces, as against some 4000 in a somewhat later Chinese context.[6] This latitude, as we shall see in the next chapter, was steadily to be reduced across the second century, both for provincial governors and also for the cities of the Empire.

For the necessary personnel of his central administration Augustus had relied upon members of his own family and close friends such as Agrippa and Maecenas, and for secretarial and other assistance had used imperial slaves and freedmen. The latter group increased in numbers across succeeding reigns; if our information from early modern European courts, in which public and personal duties were also conjoined, is of any relevance, the emperor's household would have numbered several hundred but scarcely as many as a thousand.[7] Emperors inherited this level of staff, and service was in large measure hereditary. The father of Claudius Etruscus died at the age of 90 under Domitian, having served 10 masters in succession in a range of financial duties; not only in the first but also in the second century freedmen rose periodically to considerable power as unofficial advisers to a ruler. The emperor Claudius, who had had ample opportunity to observe from the sidelines under Augustus, Tiberius, and Gaius, organized the staff more consciously by functions, which finally led to the appearance of eight major bureaus, and increased its range by adding supervision of the water supply of Rome and probably the games. As time went on, the sense that the central administration was a public rather than a household matter led to the appointment of equestrians to the great secretaryships of petitions, correspondence, finance, etc. This shift was under way in the reign of Domitian and was formalized by Hadrian, yet freedmen procurators continued to appear in numbers and were used in provinces as assistants to equestrians.

Alongside this vehicle for providing information to the ruler and issuing directives on his behalf there arose a wide variety of offices for specialized duties, all of which were headed in Rome by equestrian officers. One was concerned with the grain supply of the capital (*annona*); another, the public post; a third, customs dues (for which the Empire was divided into several districts); yet others, the supply of gladiators and animals and similar detailed responsibilities. In each case the Roman headquarters controlled a network of officials spread out over the Empire.

Italy was in a favored position, very largely self-governing under the formal direction of the Senate; the rest of the Roman Empire was divided into provinces. The more peaceful of these, which did not need legionary garrisons, were ostensibly supervised by the Senate, which appointed proconsuls; the remainder were in the emperor's direct care and were governed by his legates—of consular rank for provinces garrisoned by two or more legions; praetorian in provinces with only one legion; equestrians in Egypt and minor provinces without a legion. Beside the governor stood financial officials, quaestors in senatorial provinces, equestrian procurators in imperial provinces; other procurators supervised the extensive imperial estates in either type of province. Here too Claudius regularized matters by emphasizing the public role of procurators and perhaps granted them jurisdiction over legal matters on imperial estates. These financial directors had extensive offices; one slave from the financial staff of Gallia Lugdunensis who died on a visit to Rome under Tiberius had 16 subslaves of his own including secretaries, cooks, footmen, valet, doctor, etc.[8]

The prime functions of governors were to maintain order and administer justice. For the latter purpose in particular they made regular circuits (*conventus*) through their provinces, and by the end of the first century had the assistance of a *legatus iuridicus*. Whereas ambitious eastern provincials at least from the second century onward found it desirable to learn Latin and study law with some intensity it does not appear that most aristocrats were

deeply versed in Roman law; yet at least one governor of Asia
knew his legal literature well enough to direct plaintiffs to produce relevant sections of Ulpian's treatise *de officiis*.[9] Local communities were limited to punishments such as fines and banish-
ment; capital sentences as well as public persecutions of Christians
could be ordered only by the governor. To assist them the governors relied on their own *amici* and a minuscule retinue of
freedmen and slaves; an ordinary governor had no more than a
dozen to 60 persons on his staff, and rarely could command any
extensive archives of edicts. In the second century soldiers came
to be seconded to a governor's assistance under the title of *bene-
ficiarius consularis,* and were employed for a variety of functions
from paperwork to patrolling roads.

Rather than surveying this structure in handbook fashion it
will be more useful here to consider the fundamental problems
in the system of provincial administration. Foremost, no doubt,
in the minds of the emperors was the loyalty of governors. In
praetorian provinces the governor also commanded the legion,
but in provinces with two or three legions independent legates
were appointed to each legion; in any case the tribunes and even
centurions were formally under the control of the central administration. The pay of the troops, moreover, was the function of
the procurators, who could otherwise influence or check the
actions of the governors (but could not themselves expend funds
without imperial authorization).[10]

Governors could not raise troops or taxes on their own initiative, and on being superseded had to return to Rome in three
months; under the suspicious Commodus their children were
held virtually hostage in the capital. Their terms of office were
at the emperor's pleasure and usually no more than three to five
years—Tiberius was unusual in keeping men in office for a decade
or more. Finally governors were not encouraged to cooperate or
even communicate with each other; in case a major war broke out
either the emperor himself or a generalissimo was sent out from
Rome to coordinate activities. Yet ancient means of communications made it inevitable that governors could rule with a fairly
free hand despite efforts to limit their jurisdiction and powers.

Another weakness, at least in modern eyes, was the amateurism of provincial governors. Scholars have sought to find patterns of promotion, and sometimes are partially successful. Britain, a very unruly province, often received as governor a man who had administered a German province; Agricola had been both tribune and legionary legate in Britain before becoming its governor. So too Syria was a province "reserved for men of mark"; far distant from Rome its governor was likely to have to make significant decisions on his own, particularly in relation to Parthia.[11] Pliny the Younger is an unusual example of a man who filled one financial post after another; even as military tribune he spent his time primarily in paperwork and was chosen to bring order to the tangled finances of Bithynian cities for this expertise. From Hadrian on a civilian administrative career began to appear as in the office of "treasury advocates."

In a world dominated by the emperor's own likes and dislikes and manipulated by a web of patronage, however, extensive regularities or even what we might term professional appointments are not to be expected. Varus, who lost three legions for Augustus, had had little military experience and showed unawareness of the fact that his German subjects had recently been free. A recent effort to detect a cabal of "military men" around the warrior emperor Trajan does not seem to accord with the fact that Trajan at least as often appointed his governors on the basis of their literary merits! Another recent study of the governors of Egypt stresses their general lack of previous experience in this difficult province.[12] We are so accustomed today to the preference for experts that we may misjudge this lack of standard avenues of advancement or even of concern often for special skills; in early modern European states rulers selected aristocrats for public positions or military responsibilities in an almost haphazard style. Thus the Duke of Medina-Sidonia, on being appointed to command the Spanish Armada, wrote Philip II that he kissed the king's hands and feet "for thinking of me for so great a task" but sought in vain to decline the appointment, for "I am sure I shall do badly"—as indeed he did. It is also quite possible "that the virtue of the Roman system was simply that the varied experience of administrators trained them to be at once flexible and sensitive to local detail."[13]

Sometimes, in fact, governors were far too sensitive in this respect. In order to keep their provinces under control they had to appease locally powerful elements, who could otherwise lodge dangerous complaints with the Caesars; and in doing so at times allowed injustice toward lower orders to flourish, which was much less likely to reach the emperor's ears. Governors, again, still had Republican tendencies to act ruthlessly and to exploit their provinces financially, at times in surreptitious collaboration with local leaders. One proconsul of Asia in the last years of Augustus boasted of a kingly act, having killed 300 provincials in a single day, but usually such *saevitia* was taken as a crime only if coupled with extortion. Even the earnest governor Pliny felt that *contumacia*, refusal to obey him deferentially (specifically in the case of Christians), was punishable simply in itself. During the Julio-Claudian reigns no less than 32 trials for extortion are known; one root of Domitian's difficulties with the Senate was his effort to check senatorial abuses in the provinces.[14]

Although the imperial government assumed very little in the way of new functions, its administration inevitably increased in numbers and expense. A recent study of procurators suggests that the salaries of all officials of this type ran about 4 million sesterces under Augustus, doubled under Domitian, and quintupled by the time of Septimius Severus.[15] A well-known law of C. Northcote Parkinson was at work, but also there was continuous reduction in the numbers of tax-farmers and freedmen as against the elaboration of equestrian ranks; moreover the agencies of the central government interfered more and more directly in the local units of administration.

The Cost of Empire

The state budget of the Roman Empire, i.e., its expenditures, may be estimated at about 400 million sesterces under Augustus, rising by the second century to some 750 million sesterces in peacetime. The arithmetical calculations which support especially the latter figure will be found in the appendix to this chapter; the prime factor is the cost of the armed forces. This emphasis is fully justified; the historian Dio Cassius manufactured lengthy speeches by Agrippa and Maecenas in which they advised Augustus how to proceed after his victory over Antony and Cleopatra, and in both the financial needs of the military establishment were stressed. Maecenas, thus, put the soldiers first and other expenses second; "we cannot survive without soldiers and men will not serve as soldiers without pay." Even more neat was the syllogism by which a Roman general sought to quell a Gallic disturbance over taxation: "Stability among the tribes cannot be maintained without armies, nor armies without pay, nor pay without taxation." He might have added that the army, as we shall see later, had a good deal to do with the fact that taxes were paid.[16]

Modern scholars tend to estimate the population of the Empire at about 50 million; on this base each subject of the emperors was obligated in the range of 15 sesterces a year in the second century, though burdens in Egypt as against say Noricum could have been very different. We cannot accurately measure the minimum living standard at this time save that it must have been less than the annual pay of an auxiliary soldier, which may have been 600 sesterces. A guess has been made that the necessary minimum ran about 480 sesterces in cash terms;[17] if so, the annual charge of the burden on the imperial populace—in expenditure terms—would have been about 3.5 per cent. For comparative purposes the English state budget in 1688 took about 5.33 per cent of Britain's income.[18] These calculations can only suggest an order of magnitude and undoubtedly should be adjusted to cope with many factors. Imperial and local aristocrats as well as soldiers and sailors, for example, had incomes well above the minimum, but we cannot estimate how much the income of the Empire should thereby be increased; on the other hand charges for the collection of taxes are omitted. In the Later Empire official charges were nearly one third the taxes collected, and peculation may well have raised this figure to 50 per cent or more.[19]

The burden of Empire even so does not appear to have been unduly heavy, yet the necessary revenues were not easily raised. Almost all the population of the Empire, at least some 90 per cent, lived by farming on little more than a subsistence level, though its tax burden may have been slightly less than 90 per cent; the cities were more prosperous. Even if the Empire rested on the backs of the peasants its general revenues were largely secured via local landowners and the councils of the cities, which in turn remitted proceeds to imperial procurators and quaestors; collectors had to struggle to squeeze the meager surpluses from the countryside. Taxes were not always paid as they should have been. Hadrian remitted 900 million sesterces in back dues, and two reigns later Marcus Aurelius had to do the same; Caracalla commuted the arrears of one Mauretanian community in exchange for elephants.[20] The desirability of reducing taxation was a standard theme in imperial panegyrics, which was duly noted in Menander's handbook on that subject.

From Augustus on the main tax in the Empire was a tax on land, houses, slaves, and ships (*tributum solis*) together with a head tax (*tributum capitis*), both of which were based on periodic censuses in most areas; a mark of Roman order which is still visible on modern landscapes is the wide-scale though not universal centuriation, the rectangular division of rural plots by well-developed surveying techniques. These taxes, which were not uniform from province to province, could be paid in cash or in produce. One may assume that the civilized zones of the east produced revenues in the form of coinage, but we know that the Frisians yielded hides, Cyrenaica a famous plant (silphium), Mauretania citrus wood. Generally, however, payment in kind involved grain for the support of the army, as appears in a reference in Tacitus' life of his father-in-law Agricola; there were, indeed, bans on commutation of grain payments into money.

Pay one must; as Josephus observed, "One they obtain this, they grant you everything else, the freedom of your families, the enjoyment of your possessions and the protection of your sacred laws." Or as Tiberius once burst forth in a letter to the Senate, "without provincial resources to support master and slave, and supplement our agriculture, our woods and country-houses could not feed us. That, senators, is the emperor's anxiety. Its neglect would mean national ruin."[21]

The second-century orator Aelius Aristides asserted that the Empire was happy to proffer its taxes, but other voices gave different views. Men in the ancient world shared modern opinions about taxation; as Agrippa advised Augustus, "the citizens all think that the ruling power alone, to which they credit boundless wealth, should bear the expense; for they are very ready to search out the ruler's sources of income, but do not reckon his expenses so carefully." In less-polished rhetoric a rabbi, countering another's admiration for the material achievements of the Roman peace, asserted that they did build "market-places, for whores; baths, to wallow in; bridges, to levy tolls."[22] By and large revolt in the Empire was the product of overly heavy taxation or its unjust collection; newly added tribes on the frontier often can be found rising in rebellion one generation after receiving the blessings of Roman rule—and taxation.

As the rabbi's remark suggests, the state also levied a great variety of indirect taxes and tolls. Among the more important were customs taxes of 2–2.5 per cent, 5 per cent inheritance tax, 5 per cent manumission tax on the value of freed slaves, 4 per cent on the sale of slaves, 1 per cent on auction sales. Each tax had its own administrative staff by the second century. In toto it has been estimated that 65 per cent of imperial revenues came from the Greek East, over half of which was garnered by the reasonably efficient Egyptian bureaucracy; in the west the Gallic provinces were the principal source, for Italy paid only indirect taxes throughout the first two centuries of the Empire.[23]

Beyond the public revenues there were the proceeds of the imperial estates (*patrimonium*), which were supervised by their own procurators. Augustus calculated that he had dispensed to the public treasury, to the citizens of Rome, and to the military treasury for veterans the colossal sum of 2.4 billion sesterces, the fruit in part of the booty from the conquest of Egypt and his inheritance from Caesar and other legacies; Nero at least once paid 40 million sesterces into the public treasury "to maintain public credit."[24] At times the emperors gave away or sold estates; papyri contain accounts of "the estates of Seneca," which Nero had taken back after the philosopher's forced suicide. On the whole, however, imperial landholdings tended to increase, and passed automatically from one ruler to the next. By the middle of the second century a separate, apparently newer sector of the imperial patrimony, the *res privata,* had appeared and was immensely swelled by the confiscations of Septimius Severus after his victory in the civil wars of 193–95. We cannot quantify the income from these resources nor distinguish how it was spent as apart from public revenues proper, nor indeed the degree to which public and imperial funds were separated even in accounting procedures.

In theory at least the Senate continued to control public income, as it had in the Republic; but the public treasury, though still administered by state officials, seems to have become relatively insignificant by the end of the first century. The truly important financial official was the imperial accountant (*a rationibus*), one of whom was praised by the poet Statius: "Quickly he calculates what the Roman armies beneath every sky demand, how much the tribes and the temples, how much the lofty aqueducts, the fortresses by the coasts or the far-flung lines of roads require"—an interesting breakdown of the variety of imperial expenditure, though it omits the costs of the court itself.[25]

The emperors, however, kept a close eye on the finances of the realm. Augustus regularly issued a record of public revenues and expenditures, a custom abandoned by Tiberius and only briefly resumed by Gaius. Even if not published fiscal matters were carefully noted. Under Vespasian a bookkeeper asked the ruler for advice how to make an entry; Marcus Aurelius praised his predecessor Antoninus Pius for his "unceasing watch over the needs of the Empire and his stewardship of its resources."[26] The historian Arrian could gain enough information to promise to report the size of the Roman army, public revenues, cost of the navy, etc., though alas the last book of his work, containing this material, is lost.

In normal times the imperial budget seems to have been balanced in good order, and careful rulers could even be generous in aiding areas afflicted by earthquakes as well as disbursing presents of cash to the citizens of Rome and to the troops. Tiberius is reported to have saved 2.7 billion sesterces during his reign, a figure which is also given for Antoninus Pius.[27] The Caesars, however, did not permanently store up gold and silver as did the Persian monarchs; after Tiberius came the prodigal Gaius, after the cautious Claudius the profligate Nero, and by the late second century war rapidly eroded the savings of Antoninus Pius.

Warfare, indeed, presented serious financial problems. Legions had to be brought up to strength, supplies shifted to the frontier, and other expenses inevitably increased; in early modern states military expenditures rose during wartime from some 60 per cent of the budget to over 90 per cent. The emperors calculated deliberately whether the costs of war were worth the necesary investment; we have already seen Augustus' decision not to invade Britain on the ground that it would not pay, and his irritation at the costs of the Pannonian revolt in A.D. 6–9, which brought little return—a view repeated by Dio Cassius with regard to the Mesopotamian expansion by Septimius Severus: "It yields very little and uses up vast sums."[28]

In a traditional society such as the Empire it was difficult to increase state revenues to meet unexpected demands or to raise taxes suddenly unless rulers such as Nero, Domitian, and Septimius Severus preyed on senatorial aristocrats and other men of wealth by confiscations; another exceptional vehicle for taxation of the very rich was the demand for "crown gold" (*aurum coronarium*) on imperial accessions or other special occasions. Vespasian did increase the *tributum* in an effort to bring order again to public finances after the chaos of 68–69; various minor taxes were added in Egypt in the second century; but Marcus Aurelius, to meet his terrific military costs, was forced to sell off palace furniture and treasures (as had Nerva and the young Octavian). When his troops once demanded a donative, Marcus Aurelius refused on the grounds that the money could only be gotten "from the blood of their fellow citizens," but the fate of the parsimonious Galba in 68 and of Didius Julianus in 193 suggests how courageous Marcus Aurelius was even if by necessity.[29]

The leaders of the Roman Republic had in a sense been fortunate, for they could meet the needs of the state and its citizens to a considerable degree by the spoils gained in conquering the Mediterranean world. After the Augustan expansion this easy recourse was not often available to the emperors, save when Trajan secured the wealth of the Dacian kings; the Empire had to maintain itself out of internal revenues. Modern scholars hostile to the Empire are inclined to judge the task impossible, and even a more moderate view can suggest "that a predominantly agricultural economy simply could not produce the required surplus without intense strain and human suffering."[30] This is too pessimistic; as was suggested at the beginning of this section it appears that the subjects could provide the necessary funds, and the history of the Early Empire attests that they actually did so without undue difficulty. But that was a happy age in which warfare was incidental though unpleasant; if war became more endemic, or prosperity declined, the imperial budget could present critical difficulties.

The Provision of Justice

Roads and military installations furnished visible bonds of imperial unity; so too in less-tangible form did the structure of government and in particular the framework of Roman law. The greatnesses and also the weaknesses of the Roman Empire are visible in the degree to which it provided an orderly system governing and guarding human relations and protecting property rights, i.e., justice.

In the first two and one-half centuries of the Empire the great outburst of legal creativity which had begun in the Late Republic continued unchecked as jurisconsults interpreted and generalized the basic principles of Roman law, a structure which like English common law arose out of specific problems and their practical solutions. Augustus had begun the custom of licensing certain legal experts to give *responsa* or interpretations of a legal matter "on the authority of the *princeps*." The leading jurist of his age, M. Antistius Labeo, was "mindful of the liberty in which he had been born" in the Late Republic and stalked about Rome in grim defiance of the new regime, but legal experts of later reigns, interested in civil rather than constitutional law, tended to live more easily with the imperial system.[31] By the reign of Hadrian they often served in the emperor's *consilium*, and two of the greatest commentators on the law, Papinian and Ulpian, even held the office of praetorian prefect early in the third century.

The ruler himself came more and more to be the source of law; as Fronto observed, "The precedents which you, O Emperor, establish by your decrees will hold good publicly and for all time . . . you by your decisions in individual cases make precedents binding upon all."[32] Under Hadrian the Praetor's Edict, which had been a useful vehicle for adding new legal interpretations, was codified by Salvius Julianus; the power of the assemblies to pass legislation, which had never been a major source of new law, had long ago ceased to be more than formal; the right of the Senate to issue *senatus consulta,* which had virtually the force of law, continued, but most legislation was initiated by the ruler and his aides. The emperor, as fountainhead of law, also issued instructions to his provincial governors, edicts and decisions to specific legal cases, as well as epistles in reply to petitions, a body of the law generally summed up as imperial constitutions. All this was in Latin, which was in general the language of government, though suitors could speak in Greek or make wills in any language. Hadrian is noted for his humanitarian regulations to protect women and slaves; more generally the drift of imperial ordinances was to decrease the power of the *pater familias* and of clubs or other groupings so that individual subjects stood more and more isolated before the awesome powers of the state. Another tendency, to which we must return in looking at the third century, was to differentiate citizens, theoretically treated uniformly from the famous Twelve Tables onward, as "more noble" (*honestiores*) and "more humble" (*humiliores*).

In the administration of justice the cities and tribes of the Empire had varying practices and organs and their own systems of law, which we can see to some degree in Syria and Egypt; but subjects who were dissatisfied with local decisions or fearful of injustice sought to gain the ear and support of imperial officials of all levels. In the Egyptian Fayum Roman soldiers thus appear in the papyri as judges; procurators exercised jurisdiction over imperial estates, and not solely for financial problems. Governors had the *ius gladii* or power of execution, which they exercised primarily over soldiers but even at times over Roman citizens, and served as a court of appeal from local judgments.

The ultimate court was the emperor himself, and to him came appeals against maladministration by governors and procurators, the contentions of jealously competitive cities, and individual or group cases from provincial subjects. An important innovation by Augustus himself was the assumption of criminal jurisdiction by the consuls with the Senate and by the ruler. The former now tried provincial governors for misconduct and senators themselves, at least in theory, for treason; the emperor himself could conduct extraordinary judicial investigations (*cognitiones*) and levy arbitrary penalties (*coercitiones*) unchecked by the standard rules of Roman law. The procedure was applied especially by Claudius, Nero, and Domitian with regard to dangerous or offensive senators. Most rulers paid very serious attention to the legal duties of their position though appeals were so numerous that assistants, or by the third century the praetorian prefect, had to deal with many; under Septimius Severus it has been estimated that nearly 1500 petitions had to be answered every year. One of the most detailed descriptions of a trial before the emperor, preserved in an inscription, shows Caracalla, more noted for his military interests, actively intervening and questioning in Greek the parties in an appeals case. The historian Dio Cassius, discussing his participation in the *consilium* of Septimius Severus, comments on the freedom of speech allowed to the *amici* in legal problems, a theme also emphasized by Pliny the Younger in his *Panegyric*.[33]

When one surveys the actual administration of justice in specific cases it is evident that true justice was not always dispensed; but what human society has been perfect in practice? The rich Athenian Herodes Atticus in the second century exploited his native city, hitting, robbing, even killing free men; but friendship with Marcus Aurelius helped him escape punishment—it was always helpful to have as great a Roman patron as possible to exercise influence often in improper ways. Christians, on the other hand, were at times treated mercilessly in order to appease local unrest. It remains unclear, despite much argument, whether there were formal edicts against the practice of Christianity, but the uncertainty is indicative in itself of the freedom of the Roman administrative system from the emperor on down to set and alter its rules of operation.

The intent, even so, of the imperial system was to provide justice. A recent view seems warranted: "The air of the despot was softened by the air of the magistrate; and however bloodily their hands might fall on the great ones who wove the webs of court intrigue, there is no reason to think that the emperors failed to accord the average man a fair hearing."[34] The proof thereof perhaps lies most evident in the volume of appeals to the rulers from their subjects, who did evidently expect that they could secure justice and protection against misgovernment or exploitation; to the biting query of Saint Augustine quoted at the beginning of this chapter we may return a qualified but positive answer. The inhabitants of the Roman Empire, in general principle, preferred to be governed by the imperial administrative system despite its costs. This too was a mighty pillar in protecting the unity of the state, but we must return to this aspect in the next chapter.

Notes

1. Augustine, *City of God* 4. 4.
2. Suetonius, *Titus* 7; Epictetus, *Discourses* 4. 1. 95.
3. Fronto, *Preamble to History* 205f.; Eutropius 8. 6. 2; P. Ox. 3019 (*The Oxyrhynchus Papyri,* ed. P. J. Parsons, 42 [London, 1974]).
4. F. Millar, *The Emperor in the Roman World (31 B.C.–A.D. 337)* (London, 1977), passim.
5. Dessau 214 (Claudius on the problems of the public post); on the concept of "bureaucracy," cf. Max Weber, *Wirtschaft und Gesellschaft,* 2 (4th ed.; Tübingen, 1956), pp. 650ff.
6. K. Hopkins, *Journal of Roman Studies,* 70 (1980), p. 121; also R. P. Saller in the same issue, p. 57.
7. Dickens, *Courts of Europe,* pp. 99–100 (Francis I 662), 123 (Hapsburgs about 600), 147 (Elizabeth I about 500), 173 (Philip IV 1000 including 400 women for royal females).
8. Dessau 1514.
9. J. Keil and G. Maresch, *Jahreshefte des Oesterreichischen Archäologischen Instituts,* 45 (1960), Beibl. 83ff. (The Latin title is simply transliterated into Greek.)
10. *Digest* 1. 19.
11. Tacitus, *Agricola* 40.
12. B. Campbell, "Who Were the 'Viri Militares'?," *Journal of Roman Studies,* 65 (1975), pp. 11–31; P. A. Brunt, "The Administrators of Roman Egypt," 65 (1975), pp. 124–47.
13. W. L. Rodgers, *Naval Warfare under Oars 4th to 16th Centuries* (Annapolis, 1939), p. 262; A. K. Bowman, *Journal of Roman Studies,* 66 (1976), p. 163.

14. Seneca, *On Anger* 2. 55; P. A. Brunt, "Charges of Provincial Mal-administration under the Early Principate," *Historia,* 10 (1961), pp. 189–227; F. Pontenay de Fontette, *Leges Repetundarum* (Paris, 1954), pp. 125–31; H. W. Pleket, "Domitian, the Senate and the Provinces," *Mnemosyne,* 14 (1961), pp. 296–315.

15. H. G. Pflaum, *Les Procurateurs équestres sous le Haut-empire romain* (Paris, 1950), p. 106.

16. Dio Cassius 52. 28; Tacitus, *Histories* 4. 74.

17. Bernardi, *Studia et documenta historiae et iuris,* 31 (1965), p. 116; so too Duncan-Jones, *Economy of the Roman Empire,* p. 11.

18. G. S. Holmes, "Gregory King and the Social Structure of Pre-industrial England," *Transactions of the Royal Historical Society,* ser. 5, 27 (1977), pp. 41–68, corrects King's figures to reach this estimate.

19. Jones, *Later Roman Empire,* pp. 467–78.

20. Dessau 209; Dio Cassius 69. 8, 72. 32; H. Mattingly and E. A. Sydenham, *The Roman Imperial Coinage,* 2 (London, 1926), nos. 590–93, an issue to commemorate Hadrian's generosity. Caracalla: *L'Année épigraphique* 1948, no. 109.

21. Josephus, *Jewish Wars* 5. 406; Tacitus, *Annals* 3. 54.

22. Dio Cassius 52. 6; B. Shabbath 33b, quoted by De Lange, *Imperialism in the Ancient World,* ed. P. D. A. Garnsey and C. R. Whittaker (Cambridge, 1978), p. 268.

23. Tenney Frank, *Economic Survey of Ancient Rome,* 5 (Baltimore, 1940), pp. 53–54.

24. *Res Gestae,* summation; Tacitus, *Annals* 13. 31.

25. Statius, *Silvae* 3. 3. 98–102.

26. Suetonius, *Vespasian* 22; Marcus Aurelius, *Meditations* 1. 16.

27. Suetonius, *Gaius* 37; Dio Cassius 74. 8.

28. Dio Cassius 56. 16, 75. 3.

29. Dio Cassius 72. 10.

30. Millar, *Roman Empire,* p. 8; J. H. Michel, *ANRW,* 2. 3, p. 87, terms the Roman Empire "un Etat prédateur" (after J. Maillet, *Histoire des faites économiques* [Paris, 1952], pp. 139ff.).

31. Porphyry on Horace, *Satires* 1. 3. 82.

32. Fronto, *To Marcus Caesar* 1. 6 (Haines 1, pp. 154ff.).

33. Suetonius, *Augustus* 33; W. Williams, *Journal of Roman Studies,* 64 (1974), p. 92; P. Roussel and F. de Visscher, *Syria,* 23 (1942/3), pp. 176–94; Dio Cassius 77. 17.

34. J. A. Crook, *Consilium Principis* (Cambridge, 1955), p. 147.

APPENDIX TO CHAPTER IV

The Imperial Budget

The following calculation of an annual peacetime budget of imperial expenditures in the second century after Christ proceeds in three steps: (1) estimate of the cost of one legion per year; (2) estimate of the total burden of the armed forces per year; (3) estimate therefrom of the total budget. Necessary qualifications may be reserved for the end; one does begin with a precise figure, the fact that legionaries were paid 300 denarii (1200 sesterces) per year from Domitian onward.

1. Annual Cost of a Legion

Certain assumptions have been necessary in constructing Table I herewith. The strength of infantry in a legion is set at 5120 rather than the usual 5280, following a recent argument.[1] For the pay of the higher officers we have no information (the proconsul of Africa received 250,000 denarii according to Dio Cassius 78. 22 in the third century). The *officia* are fixed as numbering 12 persons, receiving an average of 750 denarii each, though apparently all members of a legion were formally assigned to the centuries of a legion. For the centurions and *principales* there is some slight evidence.[2]

Plus and minus factors may be listed. The legion had a great variety of specialized experts (*armorum custos, tubicen,* etc., numbering up to 600), but these, as noted in the preceding paragraph, were carried on the legionary rosters.[3] Also there may have been running expenses for supplies of diverse sorts; but food, clothing, etc., were paid for by the soldiers, most of whose pay was stopped for these charges.[4] I omit discharge costs as being funded by the *aerarium militare*.

Counterbalancing these possible additions is the fact that legions were normally much under strength in peacetime. In the duty roster of one

TABLE I Annual Cost of a Legion

legatus legionis	100,000 den.
officia	9,000
tribunes (6)	60,000
primuspilus iterum	25,000
primuspilus	25,000
4 other primi ordines	40,000
praefectus castrorum	25,000
centurions (at 5000 den.)	270,000
principales (at 600 den.)	108,000
60 signiferi	
60 optiones	
60 tesserarii	
infantry (5120)	
cavalry (120)	1,572,000
	2,234,000

century of legion III Cyrenaica under Domitian only 45 out of a notional 90 soldiers are listed; but one cannot be sure that this was the total actually on the roster.[5] On the whole the figure of 2.25 million denarii a year for a legion seems a reasonable one.[6]

2. Military Budget Per Year

Table II gives an estimate for the total cost of the imperial military establishment for a year. Again there is no decisive information on the pay of auxiliaries and sailors; I have assumed their pay was half that of a legionary.[7]

For the total of 118 million denarii a cross-check is actually available. Caracalla gave a 50 per cent raise in pay, which his successor Macrinus costed at 70 million denarii a year (Dio Cassius 79. 36). Since legionary pay at the end of the third century was 600 denarii per year,[8] Caracalla's raise was evidently from 400 to 600 denarii. Septimius Severus had earlier raised pay; we may conclude his increase was from 300 to 400 denarii.[9]

If the total military budget was increased proportionally, then it rose under Septimius Severus to 157 million denarii and in turn Caracalla's increase would amount to over 78 million denarii, which is in the order

TABLE II   Military Budget Per Year

If a legion cost 2.25 million denarii and there were 30 legions	67.5 m. den.
If auxiliaries were equal in number to legions and were paid half as much, then	33.75
If all navies were 30,000 and so were ⅕ the strength of the auxilia but were paid at the same rate, then	6.75
Ten praetorian cohorts at 500 each, paid 1000 denarii per year, would total 5 million denarii. If we add 25% for staff, then	6.25
Six urban cohorts at 1000 each, paid 500 denarii a year, would total 3 million denarii. If we add 25% for staff, then ..	3.78
	118 m. den.

of Macrinus' statement. One must, however, keep in mind the recent observation of an eminent statistician, "Any figure that looks interesting is probably wrong."[10]

3. Total Imperial Budget

Before the Industrial Revolution the cost of armed forces of a state represented almost always at least 60 per cent of the total expenditures (excluding debt service, which could not exist in the Roman Empire). To give a few examples, in the United States in 1819 the figure was 62.33 per cent; in England from 1750–55, an average of 67.5 per cent; in France in 1784, 66.67 per cent on the army alone; in Egypt in 1596, between 50 per cent and 70 per cent.[11]

Accordingly the view of Tenney Frank that under Augustus the armed forces of the Empire consumed 60 per cent of the budget seems in the right range.[12] A military budget of 118 million denarii thus would produce in the second century an overall figure of about 196 million denarii or 780 million sesterces.

In 62 B.C. the state revenues (before Pompey's conquests, the addition of Gaul by Caesar, and Egypt and a good deal of Europe by Augustus) are given in Plutarch, *Pompey* 45, at 200 million sesterces. Frank estimated 400 million sesterces under Augustus, but went on to suggest an unlikely increase to 1200/1500 million under Vespasian.[13]

Although the initial figure of 300 denarii for legionary pay is certain, the foregoing quantitative arguments move farther and farther into the realm of speculation. I proffer them primarily to suggest the range or order of magnitude in which we should think of imperial finances.

After the preceding pages were drafted, *Journal of Roman Studies,* 70 (1980), arrived, which contains an interesting essay by Keith Hopkins (pp. 101–25). Among other matters Hopkins seeks to calculate the imperial budget, using formulas in a very different method, and also the burden of taxation on individuals; he sets the imperial budget at 800 million sesterces, very close to my figure, and the level of taxation on each individual at 15 sesterces, the same as in my text above. One must hope that there is some validity in his humorously named "wigwam" theory, i.e., that "weak arguments prop each other up." It is also significant that we both conclude the Early Empire could support its taxation without undue distress.

Notes

1. R. W. Davies, *Epigraphische Studien,* 4 (1957), pp. 110–11.
2. Arguing from transfer into and out of centurionate, B. Dobson, "Legionary Centurion or Equestrian Officer, A Comparison of Pay and Prospects," *Ancient Society,* 3 (1972), pp. 193–207, sets the centurion's pay at 5000 denarii, the *primi ordines* twice this figure, and in *Die Primipilares* (Köln, 1978), p. 91, assigns the primuspilus 25,000 denarii. Graham Webster, *The Roman Army of the First and Second Centuries A.D.* (2d ed.; London, 1979), pp. 118, 259, suggests that centurions received 5 times the ordinary legionary's pay or more. D. J. Breeze, *Journal of Roman Studies,* 61 (1971), pp. 130–35, argues *optiones* received double pay as did a number of specialized posts.
3. D. J. Breeze, *Journal of Roman Studies,* 59 (1969), pp. 50–53.
4. Between 64% and 72% of legionary pay was thus stopped in P. Gen. Lat. 1 (Fink, *Roman Military Records,* no. 68).
5. P. Gen. Lat. 1 (Fink, nos. 9, 58).
6. Gabba, *Les "Dévaluations" à Rome* (Rome, 1978), p. 222, asserts that a legion cost 3 million denarii a year from Caesar on but without evidence.
7. M. Speidel, "The Pay of the Auxilia," *Journal of Roman Studies,* 63 (1973), pp. 141–47, gives a figure of 5/6 or 2/3 the legionary pay;

this seems much too high. Corbier, *Armées et fiscalité*, p. 384, estimates from Egyptian data that auxilia there cost about half the
legions' pay; G. R. Watson, *Historia*, 8 (1959), pp. 372–78, suggests
that auxiliary infantry received 1/3 and cavalry 1/2 legionary pay

8. P. Panopolis 2 in Chester Beatty Library, *Monograph 10*, ed. T. C.
   Skeat (Dublin, 1966).

9. Although one still meets estimates such as 500 denarii for Septimius
   Severus and 750 for Caracalla, P. Panopolis 2 seems decisive; cf.
   Carrié, *Les Dévaluations*, pp. 228–29; Jones, *Later Roman Empire*,
   p. 623; R. P. Duncan-Jones, "Pay and Numbers in Diocletian's
   Army," *Chiron*, 8 (1978), pp. 541–60, though the latter argues that
   one must take pay in kind into account and so winds up with a
   figure under Diocletian of 1800 denarii. R. Develin, *Latomus*, 30
   (1971), pp. 687–95, does not know the Diocletianic evidence, but
   sets the increase under Septimius Severus at 1/3.

10. Sir Claus Moser, president of the Royal Statistical Society, in *Econo-
    mist*, November 10, 1979, p. 99.

11. *Historical Statistics of the United States*, Bureau of the Census 1976,
    part 2, p. 1115; B. R. Mitchell and P. Deane, *Abstract of British
    Historical Statistics* (Cambridge, 1962), pp. 389–91; W. L. Dorn,
    Competition for Empire 1740–63 (New York, 1940), p. 15; S. J.
    Shaw, *The Budget of Ottoman Egypt 1005–1006/1596–1597* (The
    Hague, 1968). I am indebted to my colleagues Rudi Lindner for
    drawing out the figures in Shaw (the spread is due to uncertainties
    how far officials were military or civilian in character), Jacob Price
    for guidance on the British figure, and David Bien for his general
    indorsement of the French figures.

12. *Economic Survey of Ancient Rome*, 5, pp. 4ff.

13. *Economic Survey of Ancient Rome*, 5, pp. 53–54.

CHAPTER V

The Cities of the Empire

The majesty and prosperity of the Roman Empire are most visible in the surviving remains of its cities. There is, of course, Pompeii where lizards scuttle up the walls in the hot sun of summer and one expects, on rounding a corner, to see a knot of citizens in debate or women with pots at the public fountains; but equally evocative are cities such as Lepcis and Sabratha in Africa or Ephesus in Asia Minor. From Britain to Syria the urban centers put on a dress of marble or plastered brick-concrete public buildings, statues, and arches; the homes were embellished with frescoes and mosaics. Upon the leaders of these communities the imperial government relied very heavily to maintain order and obedience.

Cities or Tribes?

One very late source states that there were 5627 local units of government in the Empire; if the estimate of 50 million for the total population is in the right order, then each such unit averaged about 10,000 inhabitants.[1] We are likely to think of these centers as urban focuses for social, economic, and cultural life, and so there are a number of specialized studies of caravan cities, cities in the Greek East, or *civitas*-capitals in Britain. This tendency is natural inasmuch as it is the cities which have left physical evidence—simple villages and other rural settlements are not often very visible—and have been emphasized in the literary sources. Pliny as governor of Bithynia, for example, communicated with the cities of his province and their councils. But is the common statement that the Empire was a union of self-governing cities really true?

In Gaul a city emerged on the Seine called Lutetia Parisiorum; today the tribe is still commemorated in its modern name, but not Lutetia. So too Augusta Treverorum is now Trier; in three quarters of Gaul the formal Roman title of a city has been replaced by a tribal name. In almost all the west, in Africa, in the Balkans, in the interior of Asia Minor, the population had been grouped in tribes when the Romans came, and it is a delicate question to decide in any one area how far tribal structures were really broken down under Roman rule or their political centers became urban communities. The answer must often be a mixed one: areas on the coast or important rivers, or those favored as nodes of trade routes were more likely to advance to urban status; mountainous or inland districts far less so. In more parts of the Empire than one might think at first glance organization was still essentially tribal with only a thin veneer at best of developed political forms; even in his praise of the Roman Empire as a complex of cities Aelius Aristides used the phrase "cities and tribes."[2]

The Romans by and large allowed the natives of a province to decide for themselves in these matters. Pompey, it is true, had reorganized Pontus into 11 "cities" on its conquest; Augustus and other emperors down to Hadrian occasionally founded colonies of veterans in urban form; Agricola gave public and private aid to Britons who wished to embellish their centers with temples, fora, and houses as well as porticoes and baths, though much of this may be his son-in-law Tacitus' platitudes in order to justify the epigram, "They spoke of such novelties as 'civilization' when really they were only a feature of enslavement."[3] The pressure of the central administration, in sum, was in favor of communities taking on a Roman (or Greek) dress but not at the expense of alienating the subjects by forceful measures. As has, moreover, recently been observed the Romans did not bring, as did the British and French in Africa, "ideas of liberty, equality and national sovereignty that were subversive of their own sovereignty."[4] The most sweeping change was the partial diversion of surpluses from tribal chieftains to the uses of the central government.

Occasionally one can sense that below a Romanized surface the families which had dominated a tribe continued to be powerful, and that personal loyalties were still strong. Under Nero the noble Valerius Asiaticus, born at Vienne in Gaul, was accounted dangerous because he could arouse his own people's tribes, and Vindex of Aquitanian royal descent could secure aid for his revolt "from native leaders."[5] In the breakdown of order following this revolt and the suicide of Nero the peoples of northern and central Gaul can be seen acting as tribes rather than cities in their contentions with each other, much as have tribes in the newly independent states of modern Africa. It is rightly agreed that there was no sense of "nationalism" whenever a revolt broke out in the west against Roman rule, but cultural differences in religion and languages persisted throughout the whole period of the Empire. Nor were the Romans always successful in getting mobile tribes to settle down in more civilized fashion; epigraphical evidence from Volubilis in Mauretania attests repeated negotiations and difficulties with nomads in the area.[6] If one, in sum, is to speak of local units of government as "cities" this can only be a shorthand way of describing a great variety of structures.

The Local Population

Thus far a vital and distinguishing characteristic of an ancient city (*polis* in Greek, *civitas* in Latin) has not been noted, viz., that even where there was a truly urban center it was surrounded by an extensive rural sector which was firmly united with it politically, socially, religiously, and economically. Not until the Middle Ages, when cities were walled enclaves and the countryside was dominated by nobles, did the two split apart.

Poor villagers appear as individuals solely in Egypt, when they secured a scribe to write their petitions or letters of complaint; elsewhere the rural population surfaces only if a village as a whole appealed to the governor or emperor against injustice. The independent Roman farmer of the Early Republic had been idealized by Livy and Cicero as the backbone of the Roman state and army, but long before Augustus the *pagani* or rustic yokels had in practice been disdained or even ignored. In imperial literature the countryside rarely is mentioned, as in the Euboean oration of Dio Chrysostom or the *Metamorphoses* of Apuleius; urban views are neatly put in the summation that there is "much evidence . . . that the basic and unchanging relationship between town and village was a *non-relationship*."[7]

At the beginning of the Empire much rural labor, above all in Italy, was provided by slaves; but the use of slaves markedly declined in the first two centuries after Christ, partly because wars no longer brought them onto the market in cheap numbers and partly because rural landlords tended to shift to tenant farmers. A well-known Russian theory suggests that these changes were the root of the economic decline of the Empire, but recent Marxist students have felt that a wider variety of factors must be considered.[8] The great alteration in rural organization was to have major effects, but our lack of detailed evidence must mean that its psychological and economic causes will always remain murky; the consequence, nonetheless, will become evident as we move into the Later Empire.

To some extent the rural sector enjoyed the fruits of imperial order; the self-made farmer of Mactar in Africa, who boasted his assiduous energy, was not unique.[9] In general, however, the life of the peasants must have been grim, short, and abysmally poverty-stricken. A late Republican artisan had only a stool and bed; one peasant in Asia Minor left his two sons a chest, tools, and his allotment of land while his two daughters got 30 measures of mixed wheat and barley and his widow 30 more and a sheep.[10] From such people it was not easy to wring taxes for the central and local governments or the non-farming sectors of the cities; yet the necessary surplus to feed the armies and to keep up the builders and sculptors who adorned the cities was actually obtained in the first two centuries of the Empire.

Were the attitudes of this massive sector of any importance, and did they alter? There is no testimony in the period we are presently examining; by and large one must conclude from silence that it accepted or perhaps more accurately endured the far-off rule of the imperial bureaucracy and the yoke of government closer to hand. True, rural life was often violent, and travel through the countryside was not safe. As a recent theoretical study of banditry puts it, "Social banditry is universally found wherever societies are based on agriculture (including pastoral economies) and consist largely of peasants and landless laborers ruled, oppressed and exploited by some one else—lords, governments, lawyers, or even banks."[11] In the next chapter we can watch the central and local governments trying to keep this problem under some measure of control.

The voices of the upper classes on the other hand bubble up abundantly in inscriptions and in literature, especially but not exclusively in the Greek East; only Britain, the Balkans, and the interior of Asia Minor failed to produce writers in the Early Empire, though the main Egyptian author, Appian, was actually an Alexandrian Greek. These leaders could not command leverage to influence the choice of emperors or fundamental policies of the central government, but on the provincial level they were often very powerful; their praise or complaint could have effects on the careers of aristocrats and did on occasion secure reversal of unpopular decisions. When Vespasian, for example, sought to reclaim those lands of colonies which had not been formally allocated there arose such a widespread opposition that he had to yield. Land issues, to be sure, very directly affected the local leading classes, who were above all landlords; but we must return later to important questions involving their economic strength. Throughout the first two centuries urban aristocrats often adopted a remarkably independent position; Polemo rudely expelled Antoninus Pius when the sophist returned home unexpectedly and found the proconsul of Asia installed in his residence.[12]

In the Greek cities such as Athens and the centers of western Asia Minor one can follow the families of these aristocrats sometimes for centuries. Plutarch's great-grandfather had been impressed into service for Antony at the campaign ending in Actium; his descendants can be traced into the fourth century after Christ. Another dignitary of the third century boasted descent from Pericles, Conon, and Alexander, though this was a rather unlikely combination of ancestors. Local prominence was enough for men like Plutarch, who professed himself content to count the bricks for the new council house at his native Chaeronea, but other municipal leaders could seek to rise in imperial service via the centurionate in the army or procuratorial posts. Their wealth, after all, depended not solely on local economic activities but often at least as much on "participation in the central power or simply in the administration."[13] The greatest Greek satirist of the Early Empire, Lucian, thus eagerly obtained an imperial position as did the historians Arrian and Appian; even Plutarch at one point held a procuratorship. Men of this type shared with the central Roman aristocracy the pattern of Greco-Roman education and its cultural and social values.

The Roman Empire has often been described as an unwritten bargain between the rulers and the local leading classes in which, as Aelius Aristides described it, "The men of greatest standing and influence in every city guard their own fatherlands for you." In return the emperors supported "the well-born and rich," in Claudius' words, in their control of local administration.[14] In the Aegean world this understanding went back to the great revolt against Republican misrule engineered by King Mithridates of Pontus in 88 B.C. Initially the leaders in Ephesus and other cities in Asia Minor and even somnolent Athens had supported the revolt, but when they sensed they might lose their preeminence they abandoned Mithridates and again cast their lot with Roman authority even in the ravages of the Roman civil wars. Under Augustus, who mistrusted democracy both in Rome and abroad, their powers were much increased. In more-recently urbanized parts of the Empire tribal leaders passed on inevitably, as already noted, into the role of local magnates.

The Question of Romanization

Everywhere the leading classes firmly supported the Empire. Before taking up their ways of expressing this support or its causes we must address ourselves to an important underlying problem which has already appeared tangentially at several points. This issue is the degree to which inhabitants of the Empire became Romanized. By this term I shall mean true identification with Rome and the Romans so that a provincial did not think consciously or unconsciously of "we" and "you." This form of loyalty evidently was far weaker in force than modern patriotism or nationalism, but its presence or absence is nonetheless of significance. Let me emphasize that I am not speaking of acceptance of Roman culture, especially the Latin language; this approach is all too common but only muddies the waters. Recent students of the delicate and difficult questions involved in the term "Romanization" have been influenced at times and thereby have distorted their answers by comparisons with the occasional rejection of Western culture in the Third World; on the other hand past generations were often uncritical in their tendency to sing paeans to the results of Roman peace and order.

For the Greek East it is often asserted that there was no Romanization, but this view approaches the matter too much from a cultural point of view. In reality there was an interesting development in writers of the second century. Dio Chrysostom was an apologist to the Greek cities for the new freedom of Trajan's reign, but he praised the natives of Rhodes for continuing their practice of applause by gentle clucking in the theater and showed fairly clearly that "we" and "you" were quite different, a distinction unconsciously voiced by Arrian and Appian in the next generation. Plutarch wrote impartially in his comparison of Greek and Roman worthies, but in two important essays on the government of Greek cities he warned his fellow Greeks not to emphasize too much the glories of ancient independent Hellas lest they suffer the Roman boot. In his great oration *On Rome* Aelius Aristides always addressed his audience as "you" as against the leaders of the cities and contrasted citizens and subjects. Lucian is the first writer to speak of Romans as "us"; in his lifetime, parenthetically, the town of Thespiae patriotically sent of its own will 80 volunteers with a doctor to aid Marcus Aurelius' campaigns on the Danube. By the early third century Dio Cassius, a Greek writing in Greek, discussed Roman history from the beginning as if he were a new Livy; "his identification with Rome is complete and unquestioned."[15] Jews and native Egyptians certainly did not become Romanized in any sense, but as defined at the beginning of this section Romanization *did* take place in the east. Those who spoke Greek, however, accepted Roman culture only in minimal degree, as in the popularity of gladiatorial games and the intrusion of some Latin words.

In the western provinces there were no strong centers of culture save for old Greek colonies such as Massilia, "a place where Greek refinement and provincial puritanism meet in a happy blend."[16] Accordingly there was likely to be less opposition to the adoption of Roman culture and the Latin language; we have seen Agricola furthering this process in Britain, and it can be followed in virtually every province to lesser or greater degree depending on access to the sea or great rivers, the presence of large military camps, and climactic factors. Adoption of Latin was widespread in the cities—in Britain almost all Latin inscriptions have urban or military origins—but in Gaul, Spain, Africa, and even the Balkans it occurs on rural inscriptions and potters' stamps.

True Romans could sneer at provincial accents and did so even in Hadrian's case; a significant aspect of the substantial issues of Romanization is the degree to which the Roman aristocrats came to think less of "we" and "you." One recent study comments on "a quiet revolution" in attitudes toward Greeks in the late first and second centuries. Whereas Seneca had ridiculed Claudius for his liberality in granting citizenship "that great gift, renowned among all men," and Juvenal had poured out venom upon Greeklings, the emperor Caracalla in 212 does not seem to have met opposition when he gave almost everyone in the Empire Roman citizenship.[17]

Even so, as already observed, indigenous languages and religions continued to survive; but this continuance, or even revival after 200, can scarcely be taken as evidence in regard to the crucial issue, i.e., the degree of identification with Rome. A revolt certainly suggests lack of enthusiasm for Roman rule. In every reign down through Nero there was one or more, but after the upheaval on the Rhine in 69 troubles are much less often reported in the west. Comments about the loss of "liberty" in the speech of Calgacus and others come almost entirely from the bitter pen of Tacitus, who could thus exhibit his own particular bias.[18]

Further analysis is actually more difficult in the western provinces than in the Greek East, for there are far fewer western writers who expressed provincial views rather than those of Rome proper (as did the Senecas, Lucan, Martial, Favorinus, Fronto).

For Africa, however, we might turn to Apuleius and Tertullian, and in both I think that we can properly say that in thinking of Rome the pronoun is "we." Tertullian was a Christian in opposing Roman persecution and was led on to criticize "Roman imperialism and its theological underpinning," but did so as an indignant Roman citizen: "We are from your people; Christians are not born but made." Soon thereafter an African killed in the revolt of Gordian I was acclaimed "for his love of Rome."[19] The importance of this general acceptance/identification both in the east and the west as a pillar in maintaining the imperial structure scarcely needs stress. Empires survive for long periods only if the subjects accept their masters, but Rome even succeeded in welding a unity.

The vehicles for expressing this support were many, but were almost always connected with the cities and especially their dominant classes. Most provinces had their centers for the imperial cult, where dignitaries assembled yearly to pass decrees in praise of the emperor's protection of law and order, such as the example quoted in my first chapter on Augustus. Decrees of honor, statues of rulers and governors, and other concrete marks of loyalty filled the agoras and fora of the cities for both "good" and "bad" emperors, though one must remember that provincials could judge a Domitian very differently than did Roman aristocrats. The ordinance of a Phrygian town which established a public celebration announced that its endurance was guaranteed "by the eternity of the Roman Empire." This cast of mind was not one of patriotism in the modern sense, but it was not totally conventional and devoid of content. A recent survey of Greek writers shows that they were all essentially favorable to the Empire and slyly concludes that they "knew from personal experience what the business of imperial administration was about. In this respect they have an advantage over their modern critics."[20]

For the local leaders did gain in many ways. Their wealth was secured by the peace of the Empire, unrest by the lower classes was put down by "the dread chastiser, ax that cleaves the neck," opportunities for lucre were open should they enter the imperial service. If convicted for some misdeed their scale of punishment came by the second century to be very different from that of commoners, who might be executed for a crime for which the well-born suffered only a fine or perhaps exile. "Of liberty," says Plutarch wistfully, "the peoples have as great a share as our rulers grant them, and perhaps more would not be better for them."[21]

Not everything in this so-called bargain between Empire and cities, however, was profit. Men in the more solidly urbanized areas had long been jealously attached to their communities; even in the Empire this loyalty produced fierce rivalries between neighboring cities for titles of honor or possession of border lands. This mutual hostility was shared by all classes in the cities, as when Nucerians and Pompeians fell into a bloody brawl during a gladiatorial contest; but as the letters of Pliny from Bithynia show in conjunction with several orations of Dio Chrysostom the urban leaders also continued to be patriotic, as well as rivalling each other in factionalism which could unleash urban mobs. Neither in the countryside nor in city streets was the "Roman peace" easily maintained; not far below the surface lurked all manner of violence as we shall see more fully in the next chapter. The important matter was that the imperial government was normally quick to suppress internal upheavals and even at times from Augustus on had to intervene to check undue exploitation by urban despots. Thus the Praetorian Guard put down an internal squabble at Puteoli, the decurions complaining of the violence of the masses, the people assailing the avarice of the magistrates. The upshot was first a riot and then military repression which extended to a few executions. Though Tacitus is terse in his report, one suspects the commoners provided the victims.[22] Only in time of civil war could cities in Africa such as Oea and Lepcis or Vienne and Lyons in Gaul engage in their own little battles.

The mutual admiration between emperors and local dignitaries, in other words, existed only so far as the imperial government permitted it to flourish, and in the normal fashion of a growing administrative structure governors and procurators came to interfere more and more with urban autonomy so as to counter intercity and internal unrest and to put some limit on the exploitation of the poor by the rich. By the second century supervisors of finances (*curatores*) were being appointed for cities in Italy and the senatorial provinces. To make matters worse the leaders of the cities were all too quick to appeal to the government for support. These statesmen, warned Plutarch, should be obedient to Rome but not voluntarily humble themselves.

> As some do who, by referring everything, great or small, to the sovereigns, bring the reproach of slavery upon their country, or rather wholly destroy its constitutional government, making it dazed, timid, and powerless in everything. . . . Those who invite the sovereign's decision in every decree, meeting of a council, granting of a privilege, or administrative measure, force their sovereign to be their master more than he desires.[23]

Such intrusions were to become more general in the troubled third century.

Cities and the Economy

In the local units of government the urban centers stand out. Mostly they were not very large; Pompeii could have had 15–20,000 inhabitants, Ostia 27,000, but a study of African and Italian towns suggests that most of these were 10,000 or less. One needs always to keep in mind the simple fact that any urban agglomeration of even this size must depend on seaborne grain, for land transport of bulky items had sharp and ineluctable limits; in sixteenth-century Germany most cities were 2000 or less save Köln—on a navigable river—with 20,000.[24] The public physical equipment of a town like Pompeii is still impressive, but it can be calculated that all its fora, baths, gymnasia, temples, and amphitheater would have cost about 9 million sesterces, about twice the generosity of Pliny the Younger to his native Comum. Even in modern times the visible capital wealth of a country runs only in the order of seven or eight years' output.[25]

The cities were favored by the central government and both legally and practically dominated the rural masses of their *civitas* or *polis*. In times of famine it was not the city-dwellers but the farmers who suffered from lack of food; the landlords residing in the towns and controlling the police could "carry off all the

wheat, barley, beans and lentils . . . the country folk had to re-
sort to unhealthy foods in the spring; they ate twigs and shoots
of trees and bushes and bulbs and roots of inedible plants."[26]
This comment of the physician Galen and other evidence has
often led to a view, well expressed by Sombart, that ancient cities
were consumer centers, i.e., essentially parasites. To quote a
modern scholar, "basically the city was a social phenomenon, the
result of the predilection of the wealthier classes for the amenities
of urban life"; an ancient writer puts it more brutally, "the cities
are set up by the state in order to extort and oppress."[27]

This is a third-century statement; the question before us here
is the extent to which either its blunt assertion or Sombart's view
holds true for the first two centuries of the Empire. Did the cities
contribute anything to the imperial economy or was urbanization
over-pressed so as to create structural weaknesses in the economic
system? Here, as also in looking earlier at the imperial budget,
one meets a modern opinion that the Empire was an economic
impossibility, supported only by ruthless exploitation of the lower
classes.[28]

To assist in evaluation a list of miscellaneous data will be helpful. The expense of an inscription may be set at 100 sesterces.
One sixth of a tomb at Palmyra cost 480 sesterces, which as we
have seen was probably a year's income for an ordinary laborer.
The imperial doctor Xenophon of Cos, on the other hand, received 500,000 sesterces a year. A wealthy resident of Aspendus in
Asia Minor gave 8 million sesterces for an aqueduct—the provision
of sure water supplies even in moderate-sized cities was a mark of
the Empire not to be equalled again until far into the nineteenth
century. The emperor Gaius presented the ruler of Commagene
with 100 million sesterces; both he and Nero poured out money
to favorites at Rome as prodigally.[29]

Looking at these figures one can easily detect that there were
great variations in economic conditions among the population of
the Empire. The "silent majority" were so in part because they
could not afford epigraphic commemoration; urban leaders lived
in opulence, and the rulers themselves commanded immense revenues, but in the end they came largely from the agricultural
product of vast Empire.

Yet not entirely. In a classic study of the social and economic history of the Roman Empire half a century ago Rostovtzeff surveyed its trade and industry and illustrated in magnificent plates the physical testimony for that activity, which reached out beyond the Empire proper to India on one side and the free German tribes on the other. This expansion was not directly encouraged in itself by the emperors, but the general peace and stability of the Early Empire as well as the demands of the armies on the frontiers were underlying factors of weight.

To give only one example Arretine pottery, embossed by molds with handsome designs, was exported in the early first century after Christ to southern India, Gaul, and Britain, and many other regions. This ware was made in the Italian city of Arretium, modern Arezzo. So too most of the varied industrial product of the Early Empire came from its cities, and the commercial strands were tied together in urban ports. As already noted, magnates based their wealth primarily on land, but even they had connections with trade and industry. Aquileia, at the head of the Adriatic, had major trading families which operated down the Dalmatian coast and inland across the Alps to the Danubian provinces. Through slaves and freedmen well-to-do elements in other cities can be observed providing capital and energy for non-agricultural activities, as in the establishment of market centers in the countryside which required official approval. At Pompeii it is evident that small shops, bakeries, and other establishments had been encroaching for some time on private homes—one town official had a bakery in the back of his house, and another produced fish sauce—and gardens for the commercial production of fruits, nuts, and grapes came to occupy open spaces. Some 85 specialized trades are attested for this middling town; at Corycus, "a small and insignificant town" in Asia Minor, 110 different trades are mentioned in inscriptions. While the Greek East was generally less productive agriculturally (save Egypt) it was far more advanced commercially and industrially than were most areas of the west.[30]

The cities just mentioned had existed for centuries; in the more recently conquered areas of the Empire cities also sprang up. One interesting example is Corinium, modern Circencester, in Britain.[31] Here the Roman army on its initial conquest had built a fort in a good geographical situation by a bridge over the river Churn, on the great road, Fosse Way, which initially served as the frontier of the British province. About A.D. 49 a new fort was erected, and by 60 streets and buildings of a civil settlement were appearing northwest of the fort. The native village nearby at Bagendon was soon deserted, the fort no longer needed a garrison by the late 70s, and within a generation a true town with a regular street pattern was in existence which by the second century covered 101 hectares and may have had 15–20,000 inhabitants, the second largest urban center in England and as populous as Colonia Agrippina (Köln) in Germany; its Flavian forum and basilica were larger than those of any Roman town in Britain save London. In its museum a huge Corinthian capital (perhaps a Jupiter-column) attests that its public structures were impressive; well-cut public inscriptions stand beside ruder military and private tombstones, classic heads beside the roughest of sculptural work to the Matres, Corinnus, and other local deities. Oculists' stamps, pottery, glass, even Pentelic marble, plaster frescoes, mosaics of local manufacture (especially on the classical Orpheus theme), and a pig of lead marked with Vespasian's name attest that its citizens were firmly tied to the imperial government and classical culture. On a stone at the nearby Chedworth villa (see Plate IV) the scratched word *prasina* (green) amazingly attests interest in the chariot factions at Rome: Cirencester had its own amphitheater.[32] The impetus here came first from a more settled, orderly pattern of government which in turn promoted industry and commerce in a favorable geographical environment; if one may judge from later conditions the market region of Cirencester reached out only in a circle of six to seven miles, but perhaps wool and other products were exported to more distant points.

The common view of the cities of the Empire, in other words, as parasites or consumer centers is not entirely warranted. The masses of the Empire, as already illustrated in specific examples, were desperately poor; yet there were so many millions that a fair number did have some purchasing power—according to Pliny the Elder even serving girls had their silver mirrors.[33] Production of textiles, pottery, metalwork, furniture, works of art, and many

IV Chedworth Villa. The reconstruction is of the fourth-century phase of this English villa, with an agricultural forecourt, then formal garden, two sets of baths (hot and cold), and a large dining room decorated with a mosaic floor of the four seasons. Shown here is the figure of Winter in a heavy cloak with hare and branch in its hands. *Above, Illustrated London News, July 12, 1924, p. 74–75; below,* Toynbee, *Art in Roman Britain*

other items did attain some volume; even if we cannot quantify its dimensions the results of archeological explorations suggest that the Early Empire saw the height of ancient industrial activities and also both long-range and local trade. A recent interesting discussion ties the growth in trade to the flow of imperial revenues in taxes and expenditures, especially on the army, which produced an integrated monetary economy.[34] In other respects as well the cities justified their existence in serving as units of government sufficiently well so that the central administration could be very limited; marshalling the agricultural surpluses, scanty save in areas such as Egypt; providing centers for entertainment (both gladiatorial and theatrical) and for religious festivals and commemorations.

Even in the economic field, however, dangers lurked. The Roman Empire inherited its technology from the past and made no revolutionary improvements; thus there could be minor but not significant increase in productivity. The elements which held the pools of capital, viz., the emperors and the Roman and local aristocracies, were not totally uninterested in the economic side of life, but their attention was more toward securing their revenues and the profits of office than in entrepreneurial exploitation of resources. The lassitude visible in the pagan literature of the second century extended beyond the cultural sphere. We cannot assess economic activity in terms of modern growth theory; rather the Empire was static, exploiting inherited capital strengths. If production did increase, it did so because life had become more stable and also probably because the population of the Empire rose down into the second century.

By the later second century, it is generally agreed, the population of the Empire was no longer growing but if anything had begun to decrease—this even though the Empire as a whole was at its economic and political peak. But there are psychological and sociological motivations which can affect human fertility and reproductive urges, and changes in these areas of life, as I have suggested in another work, may have seriously affected the individual human beings living in the second century of the Empire. In the preceding chapter there was an effort to cast a balance sheet of imperial revenues, which seemed generally favorable; so too the cities of the Early Empire had sufficient resources to engage in public embellishment. But the margin could disappear; if so the Empire as a whole might have trouble in balancing its accounts, and the cities as vehicles of economic activity and government could well suffer most drastically and swiftly. Would their leading landowners continue to be loyal to the imperial ideal if the rulers could provide neither prosperity nor order?

Notes

1. L. Friedländer, *Roman Life and Manners under the Early Roman Empire,* 4 (New York, 1913), p. 285.
2. *On Rome* 31; A. N. Sherwin-White, *The Roman Citizenship* (2d ed.; Oxford, 1973).
3. Tacitus, *Agricola* 21.
4. P. A. Brunt in *Assimilation et resistance à la culture gréco-romaine dans le monde ancien,* ed. D. M. Pippidi (Bucharest/Paris, 1976), p. 166.
5. Josephus, *Jewish Wars* 4. 440; Tacitus, *Annals* 11. 1.
6. M. C. Sigman, "The Romans and the Indigenous Tribes of Mauretania Tingitana," *Historia,* 26 (1977), pp. 414–39.
7. P. Brown, *Assimilation,* p. 214.
8. E. M. Schtaerman, *Die Krise der Sklavenordnung im Westen des römischen Reiches* (Berlin, 1964); F. Vittinghoff, "Die Sklavenfrage in der Forschung der Sowjetunion," *Gymnasium,* 69 (1962), pp. 279–86; G. Prachner, "Zur Bedeutung der antiken Sklaven-und Kolonenwirtschaft für der Niedergang des römischen Reiches," *Historia* 22 (1973), pp. 732–56.
9. *Corpus Inscriptionum Latinarum* [hereafter *CIL*] 8, 11824; *Inscriptions Latines d'Algérie,* 1 (Paris, 1932), 2195.
10. Cicero, *Against Catiline* 4. 17; T. R. S. Broughton, *Economic Survey of Ancient Rome,* 4, p. 902.
11. E. J. Hobsbawn, *Bandits* (London, 1969), p. 15, quoted by Dyson, *ANRW,* 2. 3, p. 149.
12. Philostratus, *Lives of the Sophists* 1. 534.
13. *Inscriptiones Graecae,* 2d ed., 2. 3679; A. Mócsy, *Pannonia and Upper Moesia* (London, 1974), p. 226.
14. *On Rome* 64; Dessau 212.
15. *How to Write History* 5; C. P. Jones, *Greek, Roman, and Byzantine*

Studies, 12 (1971), pp. 45–48; F. Millar, *A Study of Cassius Dio* (Oxford, 1964), p. 190.

16. Tacitus, *Agricola* 4.

17. Seneca, *Apocolocyntosis* 3; Balsdon, *Romans and Aliens,* p. 52.

18. *Agricola* 30–32.

19. *Apology* 18; Garnsey, *Imperialism in the Ancient World,* p. 254; Dessau 8499.

20. *Inscriptiones Graecae ad Res Romanas Pertinentes,* 4 (Paris, 1927), 661; Balsdon, *Romans and Aliens,* p. 213.

21. Plutarch, *Moralia* 813F and 824C.

22. Tacitus, *Annals* 13. 48.

23. Plutarch, *Moralia* 814F–815A.

24. On Ostia, J. E. Packer, *Memoirs of the American Academy in Rome,* 31 (1971), pp. 65–71; R. Meiggs, *Roman Ostia* (2d ed.; Oxford, 1973), pp. 532–34, guesses 50–60,000. For Africa and Italy, Duncan-Jones, *Economy of the Roman Empire,* pp. 259ff. F. Braudel, *Capitalism and Material Life: 1400–1800* (New York, 1973), pp. 20–21, 375–77.

25. MacMullen, *Roman Social Relations,* pp. 144–45; H. J. Mackinder, *Democratic Ideals and Reality* (New York, 1919), p. 9.

26. Galen, *On Good and Bad Diet* (ed. Kühn 6, pp. 749f.).

27. Jones, *Ancient Economy,* p. 31; D. Sperber, *Antiquité Classique,* 38 (1969), p. 166.

28. P. Petit, *ANRW,* 2. 2, p. 372, who terms urban civilization "un phénomène de luxe"; A. Deman, *ANRW,* 2. 2, pp. 3–97; P. Oliva, *Das Altertum,* 8 (1962), pp. 39–46; M. I. Finley, *Comparative Studies in Society and History,* 19 (1977) pp. 305–27.

29. Inscription: P. Salmon, *Population et dépopulation dans l'Empire romain* (Brussels, 1947), p. 43. Tomb: F. Heichelheim, *Economic Survey of Ancient Rome,* 4, p. 175. Aqueduct: *Inscriptiones Graecae ad Res Romanas Pertinentes,* 3 (Paris, 1906), 804.

30. Hopkins, *Towns in Societies,* p. 72 (who notes that 350 trades are listed for London in the mid-18th century).

31. J. S. Wacher, *The Towns of Roman Britain* (Berkeley, 1974), pp. 21, 30ff.; *Studies in the Archaeology and History of Cirencester,* ed. A. McWhirr (*British Archaeological Reports,* 30, 1976).

32. *The Roman Inscriptions of Britain,* ed. R. G. Collingwood and R. P. Wright, 1 (Oxford, 1965), 127.

33. Pliny, *Natural History* 34. 160.

34. K. Hopkins, "Taxes and Trade in the Roman Empire (200 B.C.–A.D. 400)," *Journal of Roman Studies,* 70 (1980), pp. 101–25.

CHAPTER VI

Army, Roads, and Frontiers

Once upon a time the sophist Favorinus fell into debate with the emperor Hadrian over the meaning of a word, and eventually yielded to the view of the ruler. Later his friends reproached Favorinus inasmuch as he was right; the sophist rejoined, "I must regard as the most learned of men the one who has 30 legions." Equally illuminating is the phrase, taken over from Republican custom, with which the Caesars began despatches to the Senate, "If you and your children are in health it is well; I and the legions are in health."[1] Might may not make right, but in the Roman Empire it assisted greatly in bending the minds of aristocrats and subjects toward accepting the imperial will. Especially with respect to the provincials the Emperors showed little hesitation in using force to put down dissidence or unrest.

The basic principles of the imperial armed forces had been set by Augustus and his aide Agrippa. The army consisted of professional, long-term soldiers who accordingly had to be paid reasonably well. The legionaries who either were Roman citizens or received citizenship on enlistment served 20 years and then were given a discharge bonus of 12,000 sesterces or its equivalent in land. Members of auxiliary infantry and cavalry units were enlisted for 25 years and on release gained Roman citizenship by a formal document, at least from the time of Claudius; a considerable number of bronze copies of these "diplomas" have survived to suggest how highly the grant was cherished. Almost all the army was positioned along the frontiers save for garrisons in doubtful provinces such as the Spains and Egypt, and in time these internal forces could be reduced safely from 10 to 3 legions by the close of the Julio-Claudian period.

The major fleets of the navy were stationed at Misenum and Ravenna on the Italian coasts, but smaller squadrons safeguarded Syria and Egypt and patrolled the Danube, Rhine, and Black Sea. After the conquest of Britain another flotilla was added at the English Channel. Sailors served 26 years and received citizenship on discharge.

Augustus set the military establishment at 28 legions with probably an equal number of auxiliaries; but 3 legions were lost with Varus. Thereafter 4 other legions vanished in disasters on the frontiers or internal revolt, and 4 others were cashiered for mutiny or losing their standards. In compensation new legions were recruited on occasion, particularly from northern Italy, so that under Trajan there were 30 legions as again under Marcus Aurelius; Septimius Severus even succeeded in getting the total up to 33. Two thirds of the army was generally in the western provinces, about 10 per cent in Britain alone. All told the armed forces numbered in the vicinity of 300,000 men, which was about as large a total as the population and wealth of the Empire could comfortably support; but down through Septimius Severus the army and navy magnificently carried out their tasks of preserving internal order and external security. Mediterranean piracy, for example, disappeared for the only time down to the nineteenth century after Christ.

First, however, we must consider the most important issue from the point of view of the rulers, the loyalty of the troops, and thereafter conditions of service. Then we can examine the problems involved in keeping the Empire peaceful, together with its road structure; the determination of external military policy; and finally the significant questions raised by the frontiers.

Loyalty

In normal times the army was loyal to the reigning emperor, but the imperial system did not take this support for granted. To assemble some points already raised in Chapters III and IV, generals and lesser officers, senatorial or equestrian, were directly commissioned by the ruler, as were even centurions in theory; commanders of legions rarely served more than a few years in their posts, and tribunes normally even for shorter terms. Governors were not authorized to raise troops on their own and were not encouraged to cooperate with each other; the pay of the troops was a function of the provincial procurators. In the first century auxiliary units were often created from members of one tribal district but were then moved to another frontier to reduce the danger of their cooperation with local dissidents. Regular donatives of three gold pieces (300 sesterces) could be expected by loyal troops in place of the uncertain booty which they had gained in Republican times.

Above all the soldiers were spiritually bound to their emperor. On enlistment they swore an oath of obedience "to perform with enthusiasm whatever the Emperor commands, never to desert, and not to shrink from death on behalf of the Roman state."[2] This is a formula of the Later Empire, but it descends directly from the oath of the Roman Republic; and the history of the German army in World War II shows that professional soldiers cannot easily break such bonds. The religious calendar of the army, moreover, was filled with ceremonies in honor of past rulers and the current Caesar, whose portrait stood in the shrine of the legionary standards.

Even so every first-century emperor save Vespasian and Titus experienced some degree of military unrest or rebellion. The outbreaks in Illyricum and Germany on the accession of Tiberius we have already examined as spontaneous complaints of the troops against their living conditions or discharge bounties; thereafter movements in the army were more deliberately engineered. A particularly interesting though not well-lit affair is the revolt of A.D. 42 by Furius Camillus Scribonianus in Dalmatia against Claudius. This was masterminded from Rome by L. Annius Vinicianus and other aristocrats who disliked the imposition of Claudius on them by the Praetorian Guard and bruited the restoration of the Republic; the revolt of the Dalmatian legions was undoubtedly intended to spur more distant armies to a similar step. But in five days the rebellion was ended because the rank and file refused to support the plot and killed the ringleaders (Scribonianus committed suicide). The legions received the honorific titles of *Claudia pia fidelis,* though military discipline required the execution of the common soldiers who had murdered their officers.[3]

This abortive plot illuminates important attitudes of mind which helped to protect imperial rule. In the first place no other army moved to support the Dalmatian rebels; contact between provincial armies was not easily achieved in normal conditions. Secondly officers might scheme, but not always; Salvius Julianus under Commodus, who perhaps commanded in Lower Germany, "enjoyed the devotion of his soldiers" but refused to revolt, moved by his own virtue and inherited good will toward Marcus Aurelius. It was even less easy to incite the troops themselves to support rebellion; "their dominant emotion is a profound attachment to the Caesars."[4] In the upheavals of 68–69 one auxiliary cavalry unit which had been persuaded to take part in Galba's revolt had second thoughts; when the officers of Vitellius' army began to turn toward Vespasian their soldiers were very reluctant to follow and imprisoned their leaders. An effort to overthrow Domitian by the governor of Upper Germany in 88–89 seems to have failed largely because his legions balked, and on the murder of this ruler the Danubian armies, still loyal, almost mutinied against the new ruler Nerva. If any provincial army did incline toward disloyalty, it did not always raise a pretender to the throne. In 68 the army of Upper Germany was willing to abandon Nero, but initially swore an oath only to the Senate and sent a message to the praetorians to choose somebody all the armies could accept; under Commodus the British garrison even picked a delegation of 1500 men to march to Rome and present its complaints.[5] Only the revolts of 68–69 led to the fall of a monarch, but Nero had already lost the support of the important sectors of government at Rome itself. In the second century emperors faced less trouble among their troops. Avidius Cassius claimed the purple because of false news that Marcus Aurelius was dead, but when the truth was known his Syrian legions returned at once to their loyalty and themselves executed Cassius.

Conditions of Service

In all ages military service has had its hardships as well as its rewards. Discipline can be overly severe—one centurion in the Pannonian revolt was nicknamed "Another Please" because he was always breaking his centurion's staff on the back of a soldier (and was killed therefor in the revolt)—pay irregular, discharge bounties slow or inadequate; and very often the troops must be stationed in uncivilized districts, whether the depths of Roman Pannonia or the hot plains of the American Midwest in the nineteenth century. Yet overall the conditions of service in the army of the Roman Empire were tolerable, for to a large degree enlistment was voluntary.

This statement, true, must be qualified. As already observed tribes could be required to provide whole auxiliary units, and there is abundant literary and epigraphical evidence that citizens could be drafted if necessary to fill the ranks for an impending war or to make up for losses. Thus after the Varian disaster even freedmen at Rome were compelled to serve; in the reign of Hadrian officers drafted men in Cyrene and youths of the Po Valley, as again under Marcus Aurelius, when Fronto baldly urged that he "search out the skulkers of military age." By the second century the legions were no longer manned primarily by Italians but almost entirely by provincials and within this group to an ever greater degree by sons of soldiers "born in the camp" (*ex castris*). Early in the Empire only 2 out of 36 soldiers in one Egyptian list were of this origin, but in A.D. 168 there were 20 out of 37.[6] It is in this period that we can most fully call military service voluntary.

Legionaries, and to a lesser degree auxiliary troops and sailors, were paid adequately to be able to afford tombstones, often with carved reliefs of the dead soldier, though their official savings in the camp strong boxes were limited to 250 denarii by Domitian lest their commanders have a large sum of cash available in case of revolt. Their discharge bounty would represent the average wealth of a town councillor. Soldiers could also purchase slaves, especially female concubines, though common soldiers could not legally marry until the reign of Septimius Severus; there was even

debate on occasion whether aristocratic officers should be permitted to have their wives in camp lest mobility and devotion to
duty be hampered. In the dream book of Artemidorus one may
find the ultimate testimony that the soldier's profession was well
thought of; in discussing dreams which foretold loss of a job Artemidorus noted that the soldier was an exception "for he is
neither unemployed nor in want."[7]

The structure of the Roman imperial army was more highly
perfected than in any subsequent Western state down to very recent times. The surviving paperwork—duty rosters, registers of
pay and savings, orders, etc.—is impressive; Pliny the Younger as
tribune spent his entire year of service in coping with this side of
military life. Claudius organized the equestrian military posts,
Trajan issued regulations which became traditional, Hadrian
had an extensive role in laying down rules for military training
and discipline which persisted on to the surviving fourth-century
handbook on the army by Vegetius. Promotion took place along
a regular route, but only a few could even hope to attain the
highest legionary non-commissioned post of "first pike" (*primuspilus*), which gave equestrian status and the possibility of higher
military and civilian appointments. The soldiers of the Roman
Empire did not have marshals' batons in their knapsacks; one of
the few we know is Q. Marcius Turbo who rose apparently from
the centurionate to serve as praetorian prefect 15 years under
Hadrian. It was far more likely that they would die in service—
but then civilians usually did not live past their 30s.[8]

Although soldiers swore to die for the state, their dangers in
this respect were not overly great. If war did break out, the Roman legions with their standards crowned by emblems of past
successes marched out along with auxiliary complements in con-
fidence that their discipline would produce another victory (see
Plate V). On major campaigns they would be led by the emperor
or a senior, experienced general; for lesser forays the governor or
legionary legate would be of more amateur character but still accustomed as an aristocrat to command—and the long-term soldiers usually knew what to do when launched in attack. Generals
of all levels were expected to be acquainted with local political
and geographical conditions and to win by caution rather than

V The Roman Army Crossing the Danube. On a bridge of boats the Roman legions march into Dacia under the emperor Trajan; their standards, on either side of legionary eagles, bear symbols of past victories. Cichorius, *Die Reliefs der Traianssäule*

military venturesomeness; Augustus' motto, "Make haste slowly," was engraved on the military heart of the Empire. There were disasters on occasion, as in the case of Varus, in the Balkans under Domitian and Trajan, in Britain under Hadrian; but the troops were far more likely to end a battle by erecting a trophy on its site, a scene shown again and again on Trajan's Column (see Plate VI). The rulers of the first century were acclaimed in triumph at least 116 times; those of the more peaceful second century, on 46 occasions.

Most of the soldiers' long years of service, however, were spent in peacetime activities. Formal training exercises were not as common as one might expect; Hadrian required marches with full equipment only three times a month—and especially in the Syrian army, quartered in or near cities, there was frequent complaint of lack of discipline. As in more modern times military expertise could be the subject of boast; one soldier named Soranus had an inscription carved to attest that he swam the Danube in full kit and shot an arrow in the sky which he hit with a second. Soldiers also built roads, forts, and walls; they collected taxes;

VI Trophy and the Goddess Victory. Another relief from the Column of Trajan shows trophies of battle and the winged goddess Victory, who is inscribing the Roman success on a shield. Cichorius, *Die Reliefs der Traianssäule*

and they helped maintain internal order, a subject to which we must return shortly. A duty roster of one century of legio III Cyrenaica in the reign of Domitian seems to show almost all the common soldiers detailed in a great variety of activities in and out of the camp.[9]

More unusual duties could come their way as well. Pliny the Elder, in commenting on the popularity of German white duck feathers, asserted that commanders of auxiliary units sent out "whole cohorts to chase geese instead of keeping them at their posts." There is also testimony that soldiers engaged in trade and other profitable pursuits on the side.[10] Those who survived the chores and dangers of military life to retirement age lived thereafter in a position of general respect whether they returned to their homeland or settled down near their last post.

Roads and Internal Security

When the Romans of the mid-Republic drove the Appian and Latin ways southward toward Campania their objective was above all military, to facilitate movement of their troops and to tie together the military colonies established in the area. By the Late Republic roads fanned out in every direction from Rome into the provinces, and the Empire continued to build or repair roads assiduously. In areas such as Britain an entirely new system "for the first time knit together the various habitable belts in one unified transport network, which for the most part radiated from London."[11] This physical testimony to imperial unity was not easily created; modern France alone has as large a population as the entire Roman Empire, so Roman roads must often have run for long stretches through uninhabited forests, mountains, and other wastes.

Thinking of the Appian Way outside Rome we are likely to visualize these roads as paved with stone and absolutely straight; but in many areas they were coated with gravel on a firm foundation and followed the contours of the landscape to some degree; the main desideratum was an all-weather route without too steep grades. Fosse Way, running from Exeter to Lincoln in Britain, looks absolutely straight on a map, but diverges up to six miles on either side of a straight line.[12] New roads would be built often by the troops and captives, but maintenance was under the care of road commissioners in Italy and in the provinces was largely a responsibility of landowners and communities; to judge from milestones road surfaces lasted only 30 to 40 years. All told the principal network of the Empire has been estimated at 49,000 miles (as against 42,500 miles planned in the United States interstate highway system); on a calculation that one mile cost 500,000 sesterces the Roman system represented a very sizeable capital cost of something over 6 billion sesterces.[13] Obviously the emperors and their assistants deemed the roads of the Empire necessary equipment to help hold it together.

The functions of the road network were many and diverse. Its military utility remained paramount, but here one must be precise. On occasion whole legions or detachments might march from one frontier to another; while the troops themselves did not need all-weather roads their baggage trains with supplies, artillery, etc., did. Such events produced curses and groans from the provincials along the way, who had often to provide draft animals and food for the movement. But even lateral shifts from the German to the Balkan frontier or from the Danube to Syria were not easily or swiftly achieved; the imperial stress on maintaining its roads had more regular, day-to-day causes.

A public postal and transport system for communicating orders, information, and imperial letters, vital for supporting unity of government, thus was developed with stations (*mansiones*) at intervals of 25–35 miles and changing places in between; under Septimius Severus granaries were established at these points to aid in the greater movement of troops required as the frontiers became less stable. Governors had warrants in limited numbers which they could assign to officials or relatives to travel more expeditiously and safely by this system. Private individuals could use their own transport on the public roads for purposes of trade, either on foot or in the high-canopied carts depicted on tombstones; though most city-dwellers and peasants alike always stayed home, there was more mobility than one might expect. In one Fayum village-town it has been calculated that 10 per cent of the population came from elsewhere, in exchange 5 per cent of the local folk went off to Alexandria temporarily and 20 per cent more visited other villages and district capitals; on the topmost level, "highly placed men and senators cannot rest at home but, in command or under command, in war or civil or legal duty, must always be travelling."[14]

Entertainers—dancers, singers, men with trained animals, etc.—also traveled the roads of the Empire; the sick visited healing shrines, a pursuit well attested in the orations of the hypochondriac Aelius Aristides; worried men consulted the great oracles; and others moved about simply to see the world or on intellectual pursuits. Plutarch thus comments on the meeting at Delphi of a grammarian who had in 82–84 visited the northern reaches of Britain and another scholar who had been to Egypt and the Red Sea for sight-seeing and study; Apollonius of Tyana even went outside the eastern borders of the Empire to India.[15]

Although imperial literature has frequent praises of the imperial peace which safeguarded travel "from the fear of bandits' attacks," realities did not always correspond;[16] and travellers faced

dangers especially if they strayed off main routes. Disguised by
the conventional eulogies of the Empire as bringing order and
security there bubbled in reality a cauldron of violence and sudden death as men settled their differences outside the law and
preyed on the weaker. Lucius, the hero of Apuleius' picaresque
Metamorphoses, found brigands aplenty in Macedonia, and his
group was almost attacked by villagers with fierce dogs and stones
until it could prove that it was not a band of robbers. Marcus
Aurelius, as crown prince, jestingly wrote Fronto that he and his
companions in the vicinity of Antoninus Pius' rural villa were
mistaken as robbers by shepherds, whom they charged on horse-
back and scattered—the shepherds may not have thought it as
amusing. From the Balkans there are several inscriptions of men
"killed by bandits"; off in western Africa a military officer was
honored in A.D. 144 for protecting the flocks of the townspeople
of Sala, building a wall around the town, and safeguarding the
citizens while they worked in the countryside; even in Italy men
could vanish from the roads and never be seen again. Disorders,
however, were not purely rural; the Egyptian legionary roster already mentioned seems to show legionaries detached in squads of
four to police Alexandria, and in a papyrus one such soldier reports that "we are working hard because we are suppressing the
uproar and anarchy in the city."[17]

Already in the time of Augustus and Tiberius troops were being used in Italy to repress or limit disorder, and across the first
two centuries of the Empire, especially in the second, military detachments under *beneficiarii consulares* were more and more
widely deployed to reenforce the efforts of local "peacekeepers."
This apparent increase in concern over brigandage may not altogether reflect a growing breakdown in public order, as is often
pictured; increasing prosperity can lead to a rise in public crime.
Runaway slaves were often caught as they drifted by these check-
points. The famous Androcles hid in the deserts of Africa for a
time after his flight; but within three days after he left the cave
where he befriended the lion he was "seen and caught by some
soldiers" and sent to his master in Rome.[18] From day to day, in
sum, the Roman roads may have been most useful in helping
military detachments move more swiftly to cope with local out-

breaks and also in providing a relatively secure means of communication and movement overarching a far from stable, and often almost uninhabited, countryside.

Internal Dissidence

At times dissatisfaction escalated into open rebellion. Usually this was the bitter fruit of acquaintance with the extortions of Roman tax collectors and the ruthlessness of civil and military officials, and occurred within the first generation after annexation. The most famous such revolt is that of the Iceni in Britain under Queen Boudicca, who had herself been flogged and her daughters raped. On the land frontiers of the Empire, such as Africa, Britain, and the Rhineland, rebellion might also be incited by contact with free tribes. The Brigantes of northern England caused repeated grief, and the Moors of Africa raided into southern Spain in the reign of Commodus. But even in Greece an illlit revolt occurred under Antoninus Pius.

One check on such outbreaks was the disarmament of the Empire, for the strict limitations on the possession of arms in the Julian laws on public and private violence were rather rigidly enforced. In Egypt the governor Flaccus was suspicious of the unruly natives in 34–35 and published an order against the bearing of arms; a similar rule may have been issued in Gaul a decade later, and certainly weapons have not often been found in Gallic villas. Though provision was occasionally made for calling out militias, as in the Caesarian charter of Urso in Spain, or for the training of youth, the emperors did not encourage strong local military bodies. In Asia Minor even the police were only half-armed.

The most persistent internal source of military challenge was the Jews. From the Maccabees on the Jews had felt favorably toward the Romans, as protecting them against Hellenistic monarchs; Josephus also preserves a number of Caesar's decrees supporting their religious and dietary requirements when attacked by the malevolence of the Greek cities in Asia Minor. During the Empire trouble often still began in rioting between Jews and Greeks but then could escalate; Trajan had to cope with a protracted rebellion in Egypt, Cyrene, and Libya, which persisted into the reign of his successor. In Judaea there were two major revolts, 66–73, and 133–35. To repress the former required four Roman legions, ending in the famous siege of Masada, the second caused the loss of a Roman legion (XXII Deiotariana) before it was put down. Thereafter Jerusalem, refounded as Aelia Capitolina, was barred to the Jews; and in return from this point onward rabbinic literature reveals only hostility toward the Romans.

To explore at length the causes of this dismal, continuing difficulty seems unnecessary here. The tension between the Roman state and Judaism, however, does not necessarily indicate a basic flaw in the imperial system of administration, for the Jews never easily suffered external mastery after the fall of the Temple in 586 B.C.—save for the Persian deliverers from Chaldaean rule. It may also properly be observed that though the Romans as individuals much disliked Jewish ways the Caesars went farther in protecting Judaism in its observance of the Sabbath and many other prescriptions which conflicted with Greco-Roman culture than did later Christian states; Jews, for example, never had to serve in the Roman army, which would have required participation in pagan religious rites.

The siege of Masada offers a fascinating look at Roman military effectiveness. A full legion was kept busy for months in a hot, almost waterless waste building a huge ramp of earth to support a siege tower and battering ram (see Plate VII); on the night before the Romans intended to launch their decisive attack all the defenders except two women and five children committed suicide in despair. One recent student of Roman strategy is so amazed that he thinks the whole operation may have been planned as a deterrent to revolt for all the east to witness, but this is subtly to misread Roman military thought.[19] Scipio Aemilianus, besieging Carthage, and Caesar at Alesia scorned the classic Greek style of starving out an enemy town and pursued their assault with all the vigor they could command; so too did the Roman leaders at Masada—one simply got on with the job as efficiently and rapidly as the physical difficulties of a site permitted.

Eventually every revolt in the first two centuries was suppressed. Open challenge to the imperial system was not permitted. Only

VII Masada. The last stronghold of the Jewish revolt in 66–73 was this mountaintop fortress. The Roman besiegers constructed a wall 3800 yards long all around the base of the rock, and placed troops in eight siege camps (the largest of which can be seen in the lower right corner). Then they threw up a great siege ramp visible in the center of the photograph. On top of this was a heavy stone causeway, up which the engineers pushed a siege tower to command the walls and also a ram which made a breach in the defenses. *Israel Information Service*

in brigandage and miscellaneous urban riots did violence briefly surface, and even there men of wisdom counselled obedience to the Romans. The town clerk of Ephesus, when the citizens rioted against the presence of Paul, warned "we are in danger to be called into questions for this day's uproar," and it ceased. For if troops did descend on a town, the results could be a shambles. Soldiers tended to be contemptuous of civilians and at least in the civil wars looted, raped, and killed freely. Cremona thus was almost totally destroyed in 69; Lyons and Byzantium, in the wars of Septimius Severus' accession. Rabbinic authority took it as an automatic principle that the wife of a priest in a city taken by siege had been ravished.[20]

External Military Policy

The general lines of imperial military policy toward the outside world were all understood by inhabitants of the Empire and did not change markedly down through Septimius Severus. As Appian put it in the preface to his *Roman History*, "possessing the best part of the earth and sea the emperors wish rather to preserve their Empire by the exercise of prudence" and reject rule over "poverty-stricken and profitless tribes of barbarians . . . They give kings to a great many other nations whom they do not wish to have under their own government. On some of these subject nations they spend more than they receive from them . . . They surround the empire with great armies and they garrison the whole stretch of land and sea like a single stronghold." Shortly thereafter, in his oration *On Rome*, Aelius Aristides compared the Empire to a great city, surrounded by a well-garrisoned wall.[21]

In other words, the emperors were basically content to keep what they held. To this end they believed wholeheartedly in military preparedness but preferred diplomacy to war; the troops themselves were positioned on the periphery of the Empire. This arrangement has sometimes been criticized by military students on the grounds that the Empire had internal lines of communication and so should have kept a large part of its army in a central reserve which could have been deployed on either European or eastern frontiers; as matters actually stood a threat on either could be met only by arduous shifts from a quiet sector. The criticism is not really justified in view of the slowness of ancient transportation; troops marched only a little under 14 miles per day on long trips. From Rome to Köln took roughly 67 days' march; Antioch, gateway to the critical Parthian sector, was even more remote. Though the Roman navy firmly controlled the Mediterranean, naval transport of troops was not easy. Local protection thus required direct control of the frontiers themselves.[22]

This policy was a marked change, as we have already seen, from the Republican view that Rome would expand until it held the whole earth in fee. Not everyone easily accepted the shift; Tacitus, for one, bemoaned "the circumscribed, inglorious field" which he must describe: "Peace was scarcely broken—if at all. Rome was plunged in gloom, the ruler uninterested in expanding the Empire." In inscriptions and on coins across the first two centuries the Emperors paid lip service to the older theory of ever wider Roman rule, but in practice they recognized "the necessity of keeping the Empire within its limits," as Hadrian perhaps put it in a monument at his British wall.[23]

Even so military matters were a crucial concern of the emperors and their councils, who were probably as well provided with strategic information as had been Assyrian and Persian monarchs. Under Antoninus Pius and Marcus Aurelius, as noted in an earlier chapter, we can detect military experts in the imperial *consilium,* but only during the reign of the young and weak Severus Alexander in the third century is there evidence briefly for a specifically military council. The emperors essentially made their own decisions, and one can often detect alterations in policy when a new Caesar ascended the throne. Hadrian thus yielded at once Trajan's Mesopotamian conquests, which were in any case slipping away; as soon as Antoninus Pius became emperor the army in Britain was ordered to build a new turf wall some distance north of Hadrian's Wall. On the other hand the Roman advance in south Germany under Vespasian and his sons took place in a continuous process which scarcely reflects changes of rulers.

On occasions emperors did decide to expand the Roman state. Claudius proposed to gain military glory for his shaky rule by conquering the British lowlands, and even came across the Channel to preside over the final victory—he dared, however, stay only 16 days and left a trusted aristocrat as viceroy in Rome. This step was the worst military mistake of the Early Empire. Britain was no threat to Rome if independent; as a province it remained restless down through Septimius Severus and required a heavier garrison than should ever have been committed to this one area. Under the Flavians the reentrant angle in the German Black Forest between Rhenish and Danubian frontiers was slowly occupied, to cut down the time for movement between these two important sectors. Trajan conquered Dacia in two hard-fought wars, which produced a Roman province sticking out into the barbarian lands of central Europe; this expansion has also been censured, but the Dacians had caused so much trouble from Augustus' time, and especially in the reign of Domitian, that Trajan may well have decided no other solution was feasible. Marcus Aurelius sought to eliminate the gap between Pannonia and Dacia by conquering much of modern Hungary and was well on the way to success when he died, but the military advisers of his son Commodus may have been correct in judging that this expansion was not really tenable. Therewith ended the extension of Roman power on the European frontier, but Septimius Severus was to return to Trajan's efforts in Mesopotamia and add two new provinces on the upper Euphrates.

Down to the reign of Marcus Aurelius the Roman government retained the initiative in settling frontier policies, though decisions except for campaigns of expansion were often purely reactions to local problems. Force could be used by punitive expeditions, but as Tiberius wrote to his nephew Germanicus, "I achieved less by force than by diplomacy," which often involved setting barbarian tribes at odds with each other. As Appian observed, the Romans were not opposed to bribing free tribes, especially on the European frontiers; a minor expenditure of cash, which in any event often came back into the Empire through trade, was less costly and dangerous than military deployment. Domitian even went so far as to provide Decebalus, king of the Dacians, with "artisans of every trade pertaining to both peace and war," a dangerous liberality which Trajan soon retracted.[24] The Roman army in fact was consciously allowed to run down markedly during peaceful periods; when the possibility of a war surfaced, governors were expected to delay hostilities until recruitment brought the legions up to strength and necessary supplies had been deposited at useful points, a matter which might require two or three years.

Throughout the first two centuries of the Empire, its military structure successfully met challenges on the frontiers just as it had put down all internal revolts. From Marcus Aurelius onward, however, dangers were growing. Septimius Severus died at York in a campaign to cope with British unrest; the real threats were to come when both the European and eastern frontiers were challenged at once. Already under Marcus Aurelius and his co-emperor Lucius Verus the Empire had had to face this double attack and had barely managed to cope with it; in the third century the imperial armies were repeatedly to face a renewal of the problem.

The Frontiers

Republican Rome had not had frontiers, but constantly shifting temporary limits of direct control and indirect mastery through client kingdoms. From Augustus on the Empire developed ever more firmly marked frontiers or frontier zones; for no one generalization will cover all the varied ways in which imperial defense was organized and equipped with troops and military works. On the east and south these frontiers more or less corresponded to the limits of cultivated lands; the client kingdoms of Asia Minor and Africa were gradually absorbed into the Empire across the first century. Here the boundaries came to be marked by military roads which were patrolled and at times garrisoned in small forts; where there were legions they lay a considerable distance to the rear in fortresses which, as Lambaesis in Africa, were occupied for centuries and were linked by further roads to the frontiers proper.

In Europe matters were more difficult. Essentially Roman mastery extended to the two great rivers, the Rhine and the Danube, though in Dacia and southwest Germany it reached beyond. In any case a river is not a very defensible line, though it may serve well as a lateral route of communications and supply. Roman frontier defense here involved a "scorched earth" policy which kept the free barbarians back 5 to 10 miles from the river and permitted them access to Roman markets only at specified river crossings; very soon the legions were moved up to the rivers themselves, and small forts and signal stations were spaced appropriately between the legionary camps.

Modern students, who know the catastrophes which were to occur on the European frontier in the third and following centuries, may feel that the Roman government should also have organized its defenses to a much greater depth in the rear, as by fortifying towns; but the self-confidence of the army in the first two centuries would have considered this expenditure of resources totally unnecessary. The governor of Upper Pannonia haughtily built his palace at Aquincum on the very bank of the Danube.

A distinct change in the theory of frontier defense, however, can be detected. Throughout the Julio-Claudian period the legions were viewed as mobile and were housed in temporary camps, from which they sallied forth in punitive campaigns either into barbarian lands or to their rear to put down revolts; detailed protection was largely left to client states and tribes. By Flavian times these dependent areas were being absorbed into the Empire, and the camps were being turned into permanent stone structures. Defense of the frontiers against even low-intensity threats also was more essential as the districts behind the frontiers became civilized.[25] By the time of Hadrian a palisade and ditch were erected on part of the German frontier. In Britain his wall, running 80 miles from sea to sea, was even largely built of stone (see Plate VIII), though here the objective was more to keep the restless Brigantes, on one side of the wall, from easy contact with the free tribes of Scotland; in this zone, the legions continued to lie well back of the frontier, the northernmost being stationed at York, 100 miles from Hadrian's Wall.

The presence of some 200,000-odd Roman citizens and auxiliaries along the edge of the Empire had marked effects not only locally but generally. Although the troops were not lavishly paid, in toto they represented a considerable purchasing power, which demanded civilized luxuries transported from the more advanced manufacturing centers of the Empire. Therein arose a fiscal problem: the civilized provinces paid most of the taxes collected in

VIII Hadrian's Wall. Hadrian's Wall in northern England, which extended from sea to sea, was designed more to control local movements than to be a defensible frontier. Each mile there was a little fort, and at greater intervals a larger garrison. *National Parks Commission: copyright H.M. Government, United Kingdom*

the form of cash, which in turn was distributed in army pay and barbarian bribes on the frontiers; but then the cash had to flow back into the interior of the Empire to be available to meet the next round of taxes. Agrippa had already seen this difficulty in one light, "One set of people usually engages in agriculture, manufacturing, commerce, and politics—and these are the classes from which the state's receipts are chiefly derived—and a different set is under arms and draws pay."[26] We cannot in truth see fully how the mechanism of flow operated, for the soldiers' consumption of glass, pottery, and other items scarcely seems adequate to power it; but in some fashion it did work.

In the neighborhood of the major camps the demands of the army for food, fodder, textiles, leather, wood, and other commodities encouraged the improvement of agricultural techniques, the rise of a market economy, and even ideas of "profit"; one trader at the western end of Hadrian's Wall made a vow, "Do you grant that the increase of my venture may confirm my prayers, and soon will I hallow this poem with golden letters one by one."[27] Forts often had their own farmlands, but these were not always adequate to provide all their supplies or their reserves, set at one year's supply in Britain by Agricola; in Britain it has been calculated that 106,000 acres in cereal crops may have been needed to feed the garrison. This was not always extorted in a reasonable fashion; Agricola is praised for distributing the burden more fairly and reducing the distances over which grain had to be transported. In the latter connection it is worth noting that all three British legionary camps lay on navigable rivers, as did the legions of Germany and the Balkans. But the needs of the army stretched well into the interior. A *primuspilus* was awarded an honorary decurionate at Atuatuca (modern Tongres), over 60 miles from the Rhine, probably for his fairness in dealing with grain supplies.[28] Grain could move even further; one governor of Spanish Baetica was cashiered for not providing for the needs of the Mauretanian army, and at least in the fourth century grain went from eastern England to the Rhenish frontier.

The frontiers of the Empire have been intensively studied in recent decades by many scholars, both in archeological explorations and also in more general assessments. As has often been pointed out, the boundaries were not hermetically sealed; goods and persons could move back and forth in considerable quantities, though only under controlled circumstances. Yet it is generally true that the structure and order of Mediterranean civilization advanced with the armies of the Caesars only as far as the frontiers, especially in continental Europe and north Africa.

Near Wiesbaden lies a German fort, the Saalburg, which provides a fascinating visual illumination of the nature and effects of the Roman frontier. The finds from this site, well displayed in the reconstructed stone edifice, massively illustrate its civilized character: neatly lettered inscriptions, coins, sculpture, and a great variety of other material reflecting the advanced techniques and skills of the Roman world. If one walks out the north gate of the fort, the dirt path soon stops at the palisade and ditch which marked the boundary of civilization; beyond, the woods of free Germany extend pellmell to the horizon. If one goes in the other direction, southward, the metalled road is lined with the remains of shrines and other evidence of a civil community which had grown up to service the needs of the garrison economically, socially, and religiously. Often, indeed, regular towns emerged by the camps; some of these today still exist as Köln, Bonn, and other large cities. The army, in sum, was costly, but it gave security in the broadest sense and by its very presence had marked effects on previously barbaric zones.

Notes

1. *SHA Hadrian* 15; Dio Cassius 69. 14; cf. Cicero, *To Friends*, 5. 2, 7, 10a; 15. 1 and 2.

2. Vegetius, *Epitome of the Military Art*, 2. 5.

3. Suetonius, *Claudius* 13, 35; *Otho* 1; Dio Cassius 55. 23, 60. 15; A. Betz, *Untersuchungen zur Militärgeschichte der römischen Provinz Dalmatien* (Baden bei Wien, 1938), pp. 36–37.

4. Dio Cassius 73. 5; Tacitus, *Annals* 2. 76.

5. Dio Cassius 73. 9.

6. Fronto, *On Eloquence* 1 (Haines 2, p. 54); M. Grant, *The Climax of Rome* (London, 1968), p. 36.

7. *Onirocriticon* 2. 31 (p. 154. 12, ed. R. Pack, Leipzig, 1963).

8. Pflaum, *Les Carrières procuratoriennes,* pp. 199ff.; A. R. Burn, *Past and Present,* 4 (1953), p. 10; L. Kajanto, *On the Problem of the Average Duration of Life in the Roman Empire* (Helsinki, 1968).

9. Dessau 2558; Fink, *Roman Military Records,* no. 9.

10. Pliny, *Natural History* 10. 54; Tacitus, *Annals* 13. 35 and 51; *Berliner Griechische Urkunden* 462; *Michigan Papyri,* 8 (ed. H. C. Youtie and J. G. Winter, Ann Arbor, 1951), nos. 467–71.

11. S. S. Frere, *Britannia* (rev. ed.; London, 1978), p. 16.

12. Frere, *Britannia,* p. 91.

13. R. Chevallier, *Roman Roads* (London, 1976), p. 205; T. Pekáry, *Untersuchungen zu den römischen Reichsstrassen (Antiquitas,* ser. 1, 17, 1968), p. 96.

14. Epictetus 3. 24. 36; H. Braunert, *Die Binnenwanderung* (Bonn, 1964), pp. 150–58; MacMullen, *Roman Social Relations,* pp. 21–22.

15. Plutarch, *Moralia* 410A.

16. Velleius Paterculus 2. 126; Epictetus 3. 13. 9; Aristides, *Panathenaicus* 11 and *On Rome* 100.

17. Fronto, *To Marcus Caesar* 2. 12 (Haines 1, p. 150); A. Mócsy, "Latrones Dardaniae," *Acta antiqua academiae Hungaricae,* 16 (1968), pp. 351–54; *L'Année épigraphique* 1968, p. 109, an official *adversus latrones,* and 1931, nos. 36–38; Pliny, *Letters* 6. 25; P. Mich. 477–478.

18. A. Murray, "Money and Robbers, 900–1100," *Journal of Medieval History,* 4 (1978), pp. 55–94; Aulus Gellius, *Attic Nights* 5. 14. 26.

19. E. N. Luttwak, *The Grand Strategy of the Roman Empire from the First Century A.D. to the Third* (Baltimore, 1976), pp. 3–4.

20. *Ketub.* 27. 1, Av. 7.71a, cited by S. Applebaum, *Journal of Roman Studies,* 61 (1971), p. 169.

21. Appian, Preface 7; *On Rome* 81–84.

22. Luttwak, *Grand Strategy,* pp. 48, 80–84.

23. Tacitus, *Annals* 4. 32 (under Tiberius); *Roman Inscriptions of Britain* 1051; based on I. Richmond and R. P. Wright, *Archaeologia Aeliana,* ser. 4, 21 (1943), pp. 93–120, but so heavily restored as not to be entirely reliable.

24. Tacitus, *Annals* 2. 26; Dio Cassius 67. 7, 68. 9.; cf. Tacitus, *Germany* 42.

25. Lutwak, *Grand Strategy,* ch. 2, is a thoughtful analysis, though the evolution of imperial policy may not have been as conscious as he suggests.

26. Dio Cassius 52. 6.

27. *Roman Inscriptions of Britain* 2059.

28. A. L. F. Rivet, *The Villa in Roman Britain* (London, 1969), pp. 195–97; Tacitus, *Agricola* 19; *CIL* 3. 14416.

CHAPTER VII

The First Test *(A.D. 211-330)*

The reigns of the Severan dynasty 193–235 coincided with a massive turning point in the political, economic, and military history of the Empire, but on the surface they reflected the continuum established in the first two centuries. The pillars, in sum, upon which the survival of the Empire depended were all firmly in place on the foundations prepared by Augustus.

The imperial position itself was well set though beginning to be surrounded by pomp and protocol. On the arches erected in honor of Septimius Severus both at Rome and at his native Lepcis the emperor looks out at us in frontal gaze, stiff, hieratic, demanding submission and reverence (see Plate IX); but this artistic reflection of imperial dominance goes back at least to the Column of Marcus Aurelius, as against the lively depiction of Trajan on his column describing the Dacian wars. The civil struggles of 193–95 had ended in Severus' restoration of order; on his death his sons Caracalla and Geta jointly inherited the realm without challenge.

The senatorial aristocracy continued to be economically, socially, and culturally powerful and to pass on its position generation after generation, but politically it was acquiescent to the ruler's wishes; it was at this point that Ulpian laid down the principle that the monarch made the law.[1] Numbers of the upper classes had suffered confiscation or sudden death in the civil wars; the "private estate" (*res privata*) of the emperors, which actually went back into Antonine times, had been greatly swollen. Yet Dio Cassius assures us that though Septimius Severus was merciless in

IX Septimius Severus and Family (Arch of Lepcis). Septimius Severus, in an ornate chariot, commands the obedient submission of his subjects. The relief was added to an already existing arch to commemorate his state visit to his hometown. *Deutsches Archäologisches Institut*

seeking wealth no one was killed solely therefor, and aristocratic families continued on from the Antonine period to expect outward deference from their masters. Under Caracalla, however, matters shifted so far that Dio Cassius was much concerned in the speech which he constructed for Maecenas, advising Augustus at the inception of the Empire, to emphasize the need to respect the senatorial position. Equally disturbing was the increasing employment of equestrians in place of senators, as in the command of new legions and the Mesopotamian provinces.

The imperial administration, another bulwark of Empire, was now reasonably well ordered; both its expansion in personnel and generalization of its rules had moved it a considerable way toward being a true bureaucracy. The Severan age witnessed an outburst of creativity in Roman law; both Papinian and Ulpian, two of its greatest stars, were praetorian prefects at a time when the appellate jurisdiction of the post still commanded as much attention as more purely military duties. Administrative law had developed far enough that Ulpian wrote a special work on the office of the proconsul.

Across the second century jurists and administrators alike interfered more and more in local autonomy, likewise a vital support to imperial survival. Septimius himself forbade the levy of new taxes or public building without the approval of the provincial governor, and several urban posts of repute (*honores*) were subtly turning into "burdens" (*munera*). In his advice to the rulers, couched as the speech of Maecenas, Dio Cassius took a very hostile attitude toward local independence of action in many fields, but his vehemence suggests that it was still extensive; the many communities of the Empire remained essentially under the control of their upper classes, which continued to chant the praises of the rulers and adorned the towns with public edifices. Caracalla, indeed, gave Roman citizenship to virtually all inhabitants of the Empire, according to Dio Cassius to broaden the tax base but in terms of his own decree "to increase the majesty of the Roman state." The army, despite the brutalities of the civil wars, still safeguarded the frontiers; Severus added upper Mesopotamia to the realm and in his last years in Britain secured a working order which brought peace to that province throughout most of the third century. Yet one may doubt that any of his predecessors would have been so blunt in his last advice to his sons, "Be harmonious, enrich the soldiers, and scorn all other men."[2]

Shadows lowered on the horizon. Dio Cassius, a prominent senator and mediocre historian, was uncomfortable but could not have sensed the violence of the storm to come, which tested the strengths of the Empire without mercy; rather his history emphasizes the continuity of the period between Augustus and the Severi. As we turn away from that halcyon era we shall seek to assess the changes from 211 down to the dedication of Constantinople—an unusual periodization, but we need to consider not only the upheavals but also the means by which their destructive potential was eventually quelled.

Cultural and Religious Changes

Up to this point we have paid little attention to the cultural matrix of the Roman Empire save to point out the importance, as a bond of unity, of the shared pattern of cultural and social values from the emperors down through the upper classes of the cities, which was passed on generation after generation by the conservative pattern of Greco-Roman education. But now we must divagate from our major themes to survey the great psychological and spiritual alterations of the third century, "one of the most important [eras] in the history of the world."[3]

To put the problem briefly, classical culture was rapidly declining in the second century. The first marks of this decline were archaism, erudition, repetitiousness, affected style, emphasis on collecting the wisdom of the past, and romanticism. All these centered on men's inability to engage in original, fresh thinking within classical frames; later, but still in the second century, more positive indications attest an unconscious turn by some thinkers from classical culture as a whole.

There was no lack of literature in the second century. The witty essays of Lucian are perhaps the most enjoyable products of all ancient literature for modern men, but otherwise the writing of the era was affected by arid scholarship and emphasis on form; the third century was to produce essentially no poetry at all. Neither philosophy nor rhetoric nor science was in better shape. Since philosophic thought is a touchstone by which one may assess with rough justice the intellectual level of an age, it is significant that in the second century philosophy reached its lowest point in antiquity as practitioners juggled the old ideas in a dreary mishmash of Stoic, Academic, and to lesser degree Epicurean ideas or haggled over verbiage in learned conclave; the despairing words of Marcus Aurelius have been quoted in Chapter II.

The dominant impression to be gained from the architecture and sculpture of the second century is much the same as that which one must draw from the literary and intellectual trends. The famous revival of Hadrianic art was no more than an artificial resuscitation of Greek models, apart from the creation of the idealized, deified type of Antinous, the last independent achievement of classical sculpture. Everywhere one finds the same fauns and sleeping hermaphrodites and naked Venuses which fill the museums of the modern world in their ineffable dullness. Earlier local styles of architecture gave way increasingly to an uniform imperial architecture, grandiose in size, lavish with marble, but academic in concepts, though here one must in justice note an incredible breath of fresh air in the Hadrianic Pantheon at Rome, the first surviving successful effort to explore the meaning of internal space.

If there was no inner sustenance to be gained from the models of the past, then it was time to carve a new approach to the inner nature of mankind which had once animated those models; this was the achievement of the third and fourth centuries after Christ, one of the great turning points in Western civilization. To define succinctly—and so with dangerous precision—the character of these new ideas, man came to visualize himself as an entity independent of state and community. He was sharply distinguished from all other human beings and was also clearly set off from the physical world about him, unlike in the pantheistic view of the classical world. Nonetheless he had vital links to two outside forces: the divine power above, and his fellow men; for he now advanced to the capability of intimate, truly spiritual union with his brothers. So he might work for common aims in a group without sacrificing his individuality, and while separated from the physical world he was certain that it too was divinely governed.

These are extremely broad concepts; let us take an example or two. One of the largest buildings in or adjacent to the Roman Forum is also one of the most ignored, the Basilica of Constantine, begun by Maxentius and dedicated shortly after 312. The massive structure consists of a nave of three square bays, each cross vaulted and opening out into side bays in an aisle on either side. Its relative immensity is impressive, but there is also a subtle emotional impact as one moves about its great interior, senses its complex yet unified structure, and gazes upward at its soaring brickfaced vaults against the sky. The impact is quite different from that of the circumscribed, limited view implicit in the classical columns and architraves of the Forum temples. As one critic has put it, the observer is "relaxed and strangely subdued by a feeling of his own small insignificance and a sense of beneficent calm descends upon his spirit, a feeling distilled from the greater unity into which he has entered and of which he now becomes more thoroughly a part."[4] A sensitive spectator may feel that the builder of this basilica and the architect Vitruvius in the Augustan period had very different views of space and structure and so ultimately of man's relation to the world.

If one walks on from this basilica one comes to the Arch of Constantine, erected in 313–15 to celebrate Constantine's defeat of his rival Maxentius just outside Rome. Although the inscription over the central archway incorporates the elements to be found in many other imperial monuments—the dedicant Senate and Roman people, and the emperor—Constantine has precedence, and the other element is reduced to the abbreviation SPQR. Such a reversal is inconsistent with the principles of the Augustan system: that system was gone, and Constantine was an openly accepted autocrat, as we shall see later in this chapter. The inscription also gives as the cause of the erection of the arch the fact that Constantine had delivered Rome from a tyrant "at the impulse of the divine spirit." This open emphasis on religious motivation of political events would have surprised a man of the Early Empire; he would have been even more amazed at the probability that Constantine was thus covertly referring to the God of the Christian sect as having helped him to his victory.

The changes in views of man and his external relations are visible also in sculpture. Septimius Severus, as noted earlier, looks at his subjects and demands their reverence; in both private and public reliefs and statues further developments occurred. Heads of figures tilted upward in the late second and still more in the third century, as if seeking communion with Heaven. Men's mouths closed, instead of opening in breathless emotion. Physical activity meant less and less, inner incorporeal emotion ever more; one cannot avoid using the term transcendental to describe the resulting "sphinx-like calm of a never-ending vision."[5]

In literature and in philosophy it is possible to trace the roots of this great development back through Marcus Aurelius to Seneca and even Virgil, for such major alterations in human thought do not take place swiftly; but not until the third century can one see clearly expressed the fruits in philosophy proper, and more particularly in the thought of Plotinus, the last great pagan philosopher, founder of Neoplatonism. In essence Plotinus utilized the classical rational method of inquiry to establish the existence of a universal power, pure intelligence yet transcendentally divine, which could be appreciated in its lower stages by reason but in its fuller manifestation only by a mysterious, rapturous contemplation by the elect who could soar so high. Although the human soul could by itself rise to view the ultimate purity and gain an ecstatic union with the One, Plotinus did not believe in individual survival after death; as a consequence another strain of imperial thought was to surpass and eventually eliminate Neoplatonism.

For Christianity was the most perfect exposition of the new views of the world and of man, in many ways advancing parallel to pagan thought but far outstripping it in ultimate rejection of classical concepts. The growing individualism of men in the Empire was satisfied by Christianity in at least three ways: the proffer of a human being who lived, died, and rose again within historical times as the savior in the new cult; the establishment of a theological basis for individuality, to which despondent men of the Empire could come one by one; and the assertion of the spiritual equality of all men in a social system which outwardly distinguished ever more sharply between aristocrats and commoners.

The spread of this faith in the first two centuries was slow, though solidly based; but in the third century Christianity burst out into the open so that neither emperors nor their subjects could ignore its challenge—and its promise. In this era Origen, Cyprian, and many others developed theoretical and practical doctrine, often by heavy drafts on classical wisdom; the numbers of Christians rose rapidly despite, or because of, occasional persecutions; the episcopal form of church organization became well implanted and its liturgy was consolidated.

In the present work much of this history must perforce be omitted, but even on the political, social, and economic levels Christianity became an ever more important force, aspects of which cannot be ignored. If Diocletian were to engage in the single most widespread persecution, this was at least partially because Christians maintained an independent position with regard to the state; his ultimate successor Constantine on the other hand was to take the opposite approach of acceptance, again at least partially for political reasons.

There were, to be sure, problems. One involved the question

whether the inherited structure of the Empire was too ossified to welcome and accept the new ways of looking at life which marked pagan as well as Christian thought. More specifically in the present context there was the major possibility, for the Empire, of incorporating the bulwark of Christianity, as represented in its institutional form, to serve as another support for the Empire. Constantine was to try to do so; the degree to which his successors were successful or unsuccessful will occupy us in the last chapter.

Breaking of the Frontiers

We may seem to have strayed far afield from our normal frame of reference into areas which commonly receive no attention in discussions of the third-century chaos, but intellectual and spiritual mutations may have at least as great influence on historical revolutions as more mundane political and military developments. In surveying the third century it may also be useful, and perhaps comforting, to realize that the period was one of truly great advances as well as dismal upheavals. At all events we must return, in Tacitean phrase, to themes "narrow and inglorious."[6]

Troubles in an Empire often show themselves first on its fringes, the sensitive zone between order and barbarity, though the causes of these difficulties may lie far in the interior as well as among the free peoples beyond imperial sway (see Map 2). One of the most obvious signs of distress in the third century thus is the repeated collapse of frontier defenses.

The detailed account of enemy invasions during the period need not concern us here, and in any event that history can hardly be recovered in a meaningful way. After Dio Cassius and Herodian laid down their pens in the early decades of the century we have as literary guides only the miserable Augustan History, a collection of imperial biographies down through Carus, and brief surveys in fourth-century epitomes of Roman history. Inscriptions, coinage, and archeological material also slope off very rapidly after the Severan period. It is all too easy to lay this decline onto the disruptions of the era, but even in areas not directly beset a hiatus is evident in our physical testimony.

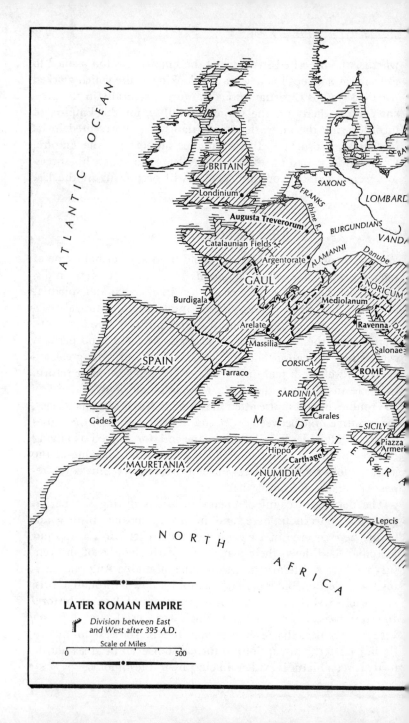

ATLANTIC OCEAN

BRITAIN

Londinium

SAXONS

LOMBARD

FRANKS

Rhine R.

Augusta Treverorum

BURGUNDIANS

VAND

Catalaunian Fields

ALAMANNI

Danube

Argentorate

NORICUM

GAUL

Burdigala

Mediolanum

Ravenna

Arelate

Salonae

Massilia

CORSICA

ROME

SPAIN

Tarraco

SARDINIA

Gades

Carales

SICILY

Piazza
Armeri

M E D I T E R A

Hippo

Carthage

MAURETANIA

NUMIDIA

Lepcis

NORTH

AFRICA

LATER ROMAN EMPIRE

Division between East
and West after 395 A.D.

Scale of Miles

0   500

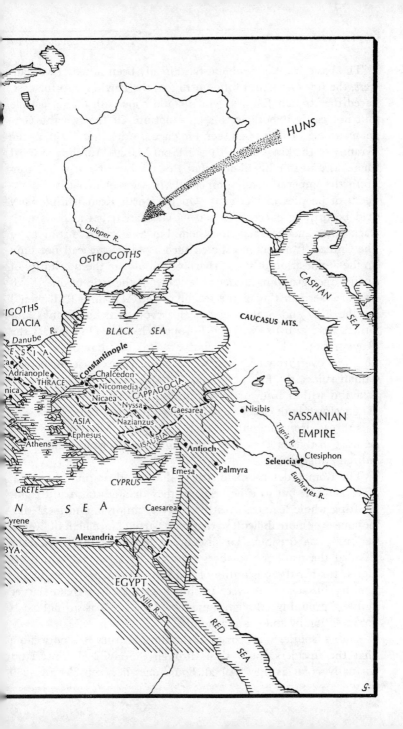

The basic frontier problem has already been noted. Two dangers, the free Germans to the north and the Parthians to the east, faced the Roman Empire, which could cope with one at a time but not easily if both were set in motion. Of the two the Germans were as Tacitus had seen long ago, a "deadlier foe than the tyranny of the kings of Parthia."[7] From Marcus Aurelius onward there was greater likelihood that this double threat would confront the imperial armies, especially in view of extensive movement of peoples in Germany. On the north Roman diplomacy had been quite effective in setting German tribes at odds with each other and in fracturing them, but as a sensitive student of the Chinese frontiers has shown such a policy can lead not only to the atomization of the barbarians but also to the possibility of their larger grouping under able leaders;[8] the title of one third-century German threat, the league of the Alamanni ("all men") on the Elbe and Saale, suggests this evolution, but Franks and others were also to assail the European legions. On the east the Roman Empire had faced a relatively weak Parthian dynasty; but this was overthrown by a new, far more vigorous series of Sassanian rulers, the first of whom, Ardashir, was crowned king in 226 and within four years was attacking Roman Mesopotamia. Thenceforth both eastern and northern frontiers faced more serious threats from the outside than had been previously true, and at least in the Balkans internal dissidence also compounded the military difficulties.

The Roman defenses had still in the second century been relatively supple, but as time went on they became static and rigid. Shifting whole legions, with their wives, children, and local ties, became ever more difficult so that only partial movement of "vexillations" was feasible. To discourage revolt Septimius Severus divided the frontier provinces into smaller segments, which reduced further the possibility of coordinated defense; later in the century his successors were to find it necessary to create larger military groupings, though these served too often as springboards for rebellion by ambitious generals.

Once a frontier was broken in the third century it is noticeable that the invaders could slice through the civilized hinterland virtually as far as they wished. Four times between 254 and 280 the Germans erupted across the Rhine; their route of advance as far as Spain and even Africa is marked by the hundreds of coin hoards buried in this period by men who did not live to reclaim their wealth. Here as elsewhere the barbarians were ruthless; the third-century bishop Gregory Thaumaturgus of Asia Minor laid down rules how to treat raped virgins, those who lost their property and so robbed others, those who abetted the enemy to gain booty or save their lives.[9] In the Balkans the Goths began by attacking Greek cities on the Black Sea from 238 on and with the Heruli launched naval expeditions between 253 and 269 which drove down into the Aegean as far as Athens and Corinth and plundered the peaceful cities of Ionia. On the east war with the Sassanians resulted in 260 in the capture of the emperor Valerian, the only Roman ruler ever to fall into the enemy's hands; thereafter the Sassanian army took the eastern metropolis of Antioch and thrust far into Asia Minor.

It is not entirely correct to say the Caesars of the first two centuries after Christ deliberately and totally disarmed the interior provinces, but certainly the possibilities of local defence against these invasions had been greatly weakened. Here and there, nonetheless, spontaneous opposition did have some role. The Athenian historian Dexippus pulled together enough military strength to check the Heruli in central Greece; in Asia Minor the Sassanian incursion was also limited by another leader, Callistus, an imperial military official who rallied local forces. These examples come from the east; we hear of no similar reactions in the threatened western provinces.

What was the Empire to do in coping with this internal situation or in restoring the frontiers themselves? One solution was to encourage the walling of towns; and so in Gaul, for example, communities shrank appreciably in size in order to ease the burden of walling their enceintes. Even Rome was given the brick/concrete wall by Aurelian which still stands in many stretches, though this was conceived on a far larger scale. On the frontiers themselves forts and fortlets were built on good defensive sites as resources permitted, in a deeper zone so that their garrisons could limit or threaten the rear of penetrations; most German tribes were not yet prepared for formal sieges.

More important was the reorganization of the army itself to provide an elastic defense which "would at least ensure the ultimate security of the imperial power (though not of imperial *territory*)."[10] The Roman army had always had more cavalry than is sometimes recognized; this arm has been estimated at some 80,000 in the second century but was grouped in small cavalry or mixed cavalry/infantry units. Especially under Gallienus the cavalry component seems to have been enlarged and pulled together as a mobile corps, the more effective inasmuch as the Germans moved and fought on foot. A growing division between internal strategic, mobile forces and static frontier elements, which is quite visible in the fourth century, was already appearing in the third, though this process resulted overall in an expensive and dangerous enlargement of the military component of the Empire.

Perhaps most significant was a possibly conscious decision to concentrate imperial military energies rather than dissipating them. After Gallienus the Roman emperors left the Rhenish frontier to the care of the local usurpers of the Imperium Galliarum for well over a decade; they even removed troops for other sectors on several occasions, each time leading to one of the greater German invasions. On the other hand the emperors sought earnestly to protect north Italy and were often to be found on the Danubian frontier. Both they and major elements of their mobile forces had Balkan origins from the middle of the century; more important the great line of land communication between east and west along which rulers and troops scurried to meet Pannonian and Sassanian threats simply had to be protected. So too imperial attention was devoted to the defense of the eastern provinces. Initial Sassanian triumphs had resulted in the loss of the Severan acquisitions in upper Mesopotamia, but before the end of the century these had been regained and the emperors Carus and Galerius both thrust as far as the Sassanian lowland capital of Ctesiphon.

By the reign of Diocletian the frontiers had been restored, apart from the cession of Dacia, the reentrant German angle in the Black Forest, and some fringe areas in Africa; the Empire "without end" was shrinking. Discipline had sometimes broken down so far that Roman soldiers deserted to the enemy, and considerable numbers of barbarians had been incorporated in military units; still, the Roman army retained an advantage in training and deliberate planning as against especially the German tribes, which were dangerous in initial rush but lacked cohesiveness and civilized, methodical determination. By legal or illegal means the Roman troops could secure the supplies of food, transport animals, and other essentials of war, though the devastating effects of these demands will concern us in following pages. Above all the sheer necessities of these dangerous times forced the elevation of mature, able leaders. Even the pitiful Severus Alexander commanded in person his wars in Mesopotamia and on the Rhine; Gordian III had had to leave Rome to wage his eastern war in vain, but the restoration of order by Diocletian and his aides was founded far more on the achievements of men such as Claudius II Gothicus, Probus, and above all the stern figure of Aurelian, nicknamed "Hand on Hilt."

Nor were all areas of the Empire equally beset by external troubles. The province of Britain was tranquil through at least the first half of the third century; so too the African provinces began really to burgeon late in the second century and by and large throve in the third. As Adam Smith once said, "There is a lot of ruin in a country," i.e., inherited resources cannot be dissipated in one moment or generation. The imperial fiscal and administrative system was very heavily tested in the third century—and not solely because of frontier problems—but it was not broken even though the toll on the civil population was heavy, as was also the stress on inherited balances of government and society.

The Imperial Merry-Go-Round

After Septimius Severus his successors in the Severan dynasty were the most contemptible group ever to wear the purple down to the figureheads in the fifth-century western Empire. His heirs were his sons Caracalla and Geta; the elder soon got rid of his brother by assassination in their mother's lap. Dio Cassius asserts that Caracalla was not educated, but this seems most unlikely in view of the usual training of crown princes in classical culture; Caracalla was articulate enough in the detailed report of a judicial hearing in 216 and listened, like his predecessors, to the flowing phrases of rhetorical eulogists. Still, in his reign he showed awareness of the past primarily in his remarkable efforts to ape Alexander and otherwise preferred the life of the camp.

On his murder the praetorian prefect Macrinus seized the throne for eighteen months, the first equestrian to be emperor and also the first not to visit Rome during his rule. After this interval came M. Aurelius Antoninus, better known as Elagabalus because of his extravagant worship of this Syrian deity and otherwise so perverted as to fill Dio Cassius with horror. Eventually he was set aside for his cousin Severus Alexander, who ruled weakly down to 235, giving as a consequence more voice to the senatorial aristocracy than had been common. Had not the dynasty been blessed by a series of strong-minded wives and mothers (often named Julia) it would scarcely have lasted as long as it did, but that very endurance suggests how firmly the dynastic principle of imperial succession was implanted in men's minds.

In 235 the generals on the Rhine contemptuously removed Severus Alexander and elevated Maximinus Thrax, who had risen from the ranks and had almost no share in the classical tradition. Thereafter the Empire had no more dynasties in the third century.

Sometimes Septimius Severus has been held responsible, through his severity and confiscations, for the deterioration which led to the Decline and Fall, an example of the unfortunate historical tendency to anchor causes in specific individuals; far more devastating were the inadequacies of his successors, who destroyed the image of the imperial role built up in the previous two centuries. Thenceforth ambitious generals and praetorian prefects, as well as the troops, felt far freer to venture the gamble of seizing power. Something, too, must be allowed to the pressure of the frontier wars, which both prevented emperors from watching their governors and also gave impetus to ambitious, successful commanders. This disastrous combination of disruptive factors led to the result, totally inexplicable in terms of the strong imperial position of earlier centuries, that from 235 to 284 there were no less than 21 emperors (see Table of Emperors) and almost as many unsuccessful claimants. In 260 the Gallic provinces together with Britain broke away in a separate Imperium Galliarum; so too the eastern provinces became independent under the leadership of the lords of Palmyra. The scourges of external invasions and internal civil war combined to lacerate the body politic.

In Chapter II we isolated three principal requirements for imperial survival: support by the entourage of the emperor including the Praetorian Guard, acceptance by the armies generally, and endorsement by the senatorial aristocracy. Though the Roman mobs rioted again and again in the third century and even supported a revolt under Aurelian, their effectiveness in unseating rulers remained as nugatory as in earlier centuries; the major change in the three factors just listed was the loss of power by the senatorial aristocracy.

This group acted in a significant way for the last time in connection with the overthrow of Maximinus Thrax. First the aged proconsul of Africa, Gordian I, the richest aristocrat of the age, claimed the purple together with his son; though this rebellion, which had only the youths of Carthage to support it, was easily quashed by the neighboring legate of Numidia with his legion III Augusta, the Senate in Rome had already condemned the semi-barbarian Maximinus and desperately set up a board of 20 commissioners to lead an Italian revolt. Its heads Pupienus and Balbinus recruited the young men of Italy; the city of Aquileia resisted a siege by Maximinus; and perhaps to everyone's surprise his own soldiers turned against him and killed both Maximinus and his son. The Praetorian Guard, however, soon despatched Pupienus and Balbinus so that Gordian III, grandson of the African rebel, became sole ruler at the age of 13. His all-powerful praetorian prefect Timestheus sought to protect the aristocracy to some degree, but thereafter it retreated farther and farther into the political background; Gallienus even removed its members from command over armies and at least some provinces. In any case great landowners may already have decided in large measure to abandon public office for individual safety; after 282 the Senate was not even expected to confer official recognition on a new ruler.

Equestrians thus reached the height of their power in imperial history. Outwardly the administration of the Empire became steadily militarized in dress and manner, and soldiers were more widely employed in essentially civil functions; but the repeated view in disturbed historical times that one can rely on the army as "the last intact social body in a disintegrating society" is as erroneous for the third century as for any modern era.[11] In the next chapter we shall return to the actual nature of the army in the third and following centuries.

Let us count our emperors. From the accession of Gordian III to that of Diocletian two Caesars (Claudius and the aged Tacitus, actually chosen by the Senate on the murder of Aurelian) died natural deaths; one (Decius) was killed in a frontier battle, and another (Valerian) was taken prisoner by the Sassanians. All the rest fell prey to their headquarters staff, usually abetted by ambitious praetorian prefects, or in civil war. The latter, however, must not be exaggerated. Decius defeated Philip in open battle, so too Diocletian against Carinus; but Gallus, Aemilianus, and Quintillus all committed suicide in despair or were killed by their own troops.

Some 17 serious plotters or pretenders to the throne—omitting the masters of the Imperium Galliarum who called themselves emperors—must also be taken into account; almost every reign saw one or more uprising. A number of these figures are only names, and their fates unknown; most of the rest were eliminated by their own aides or troops when their situation could be seen as hopeless. But several had to be dealt with on the battlefield. The imperial position, in sum, was an insecure one, though this was not the primary cause for internal changes; we hear very little of confiscations and executions, unlike the ruthless procedure of Septimius Severus on his victories 193–95.

Throughout the period of imperial instability the primary activity of any ruler was a desperate effort to secure the loyalty of the armies, which is marked by the concentration of coin legends on Concord, Faith of the Troops, and other types. Thereafter defense of the frontiers absorbed almost all their energies; the main further claim on their coinage is "restoration" of order.[12] For Probus we hear of efforts to improve the fertility of the Balkan countryside, labors which so angered his troops that they rebelled; Gallienus occupies an unusual position in promoting the activities of the philosopher Plotinus, who even dreamed of establishing a model city in Campania; Aurelian sought to reform the currency. But essentially the economic and political evolution of the third-century Empire took place unchecked and unguided.

City and Countryside

In turning to these areas we enter a very murky field, and precision is not always easily attained; the changes of the third century are to be assessed only with caution. Generally, however, there is agreement that the population declined steadily after the middle of the second century and that this process perhaps accelerated in the third century; the plagues recorded in our scanty sources, barbarian invasions, and civil wars, however, certainly had only minor effect in abetting this change. Since overall production depended primarily on the number of producers, the output of manufactured goods as well as trade therein would also have decreased; archeological testimony graphically supports this inference and indeed suggests that the industrial and commercial deterioration of imperial life was extremely severe. Here and there spasmodically in third-century literature a sense of gloom can be detected, though often in a Christian moral context, as in Cyprian's complaints about anarchy, inflation, class conflict, lack of manpower, and other ills.[13]

Yet the needs of the state did not decrease, even though public building at Rome and in the cities came to a virtual halt (apart from urban walls). The numbers of troops rose, and their requirements became more burdensome as they moved in detachments about the Empire; each new ruler, moreover, had to reward his armies by accession gifts. Already in the second century an inscription from Mauretania explicitly commented that the soldiers came first; this priority was not yielded by the emperor-making armies of the third century.[14]

In earlier periods military supply of grain (*annona*) and transport (*angareia*) has been assured by established procedures, though as in the case of Agricola in Britain this supply had at times been accompanied by extortion and even mismanagement. In the breakdown of public order in the third century the difficulties were compounded, and both *annona* and *angareia* were exacted by military units without much regard to legality. Often grain was commandeered directly rather than through the intermediary vehicle of taxation and payment therefor in cash, though the *annona* never became a true tax in itself.

Despite tendencies to revert toward a natural economy the public structure of the Empire continued to be based on coinage, so much so that Septimius Severus had firmly laid down once again the principle that "we have forbidden that you pay money in place of grain." Egyptian papyri still reckoned in currency though economic activity in the cities seems to have made less use of actual money. At least once Egyptian banks closed in refusal "to accept the divine coin of the Emperors" and had to be commanded "to accept and change all coin except what is clearly spurious and counterfeit."[15] The voluminous copper coinage of the eastern cities, some 295 in Asia Minor alone, came to a halt by the later third century.

Here arose difficulties which have much interested modern economic historians. To some degree taxes could be raised or new imposts demanded of the subjects; thus "crown gold" was more often demanded from the aristocracy from Caracalla on, who also doubled emancipation and inheritance taxes (reduced again by Macrinus). From the time of Marcus Aurelius rulers found it insidiously easier to inflate the currency by lowering the silver content of the standard *denarius*—gold was not thus adulterated, partly because it was paid in subsidy to barbarian tribes or otherwise dispensed to recipients who could successfully object to debasement. The details of this silver depreciation have been followed out carefully by numismatists; in the time of Marcus Aurelius the *denarius* was 75 per cent silver, under Septimius Severus 50 per cent, and by the reign of Gallienus so-called silver coins had only a wash of silver, less than 5 per cent of the weight of the coin. The volume of such coinage increased seven times from 238 to 274.[16] The inevitable result was a runaway price increase, which began to be severe from about 260 onward to judge from Egyptian and rabbinic records.

The effects of depreciation combined with inflation were lamentable and not only in the private sector; "discrimination

against the public services is an organic feature of inflation."[17]
Yet it must be kept in mind the element most directly affected
was the urban population. Most of the peasantry lived essentially on a subsistence level and so was not immediately touched,
though what happened in the cities inevitably eddied out into
the surrounding countryside. When combined with the decline
in manufacture and trade, however, the position of the cities became parlous indeed.

During the first two centuries of the Empire the emphasis of
imperial administration had been on promoting the growth of
urban centers and granting their leading classes a considerable
degree of autonomy. Toward the end of the second century the
jurists elaborated a theory of *origo,* i.e., that every inhabitant of
the Empire had a specific attachment which he, by inference, was
expected to support.

During the third century, on the other hand, the great economic and social historian Rostovtzeff found a decisive shift as
the emperors joined forces with the lower classes (especially as
represented in the soldiery) against the urban upper classes. This
theory has been carefully examined during the past half century
and is now generally rejected. If the soldiers pillaged local upper
classes, this reflects both a decline in discipline and the evident
fact that the cities were most worth attacking. Yet in the end
Rostovtzeff was not totally in error, for in the third century the
central government did put heavier and heavier pressure on the
members of town councils (the *curiales,* as they were now called).
Their autonomy was much reduced by the spread of imperial officials such as *curatores* and *correctors* to control finances; their
responsibilities in tax collections were ruthlessly enforced, and
when leading families sought to avoid the position of *curialis*
they were dragooned into office. An incidental but telling reflection of the results appears in the advice of one rabbi, anent the
general ban on Jews leaving Palestine for economic reasons, "If
they have nominated you for the council, let the Jordan be your
frontier," i.e., flee abroad.[18]

In many ways, thus, the position of the cities deteriorated
though not by conscious imperial desire. The blunt facts were
that the army and the aristocracy were too powerful to be made

X Rural Life in the Late Empire. The late fourth-century mosaic picture of the rural estate of Lord Julius (so named in the lower right corner) was found at Carthage. In the four corners the gifts of the estate in the four seasons are presented to the master and mistress to attest

to bear the brunt of imperial demands, the peasantry too diffuse and poor, but the urban upper classes directly open to central administrative pressures. If cities had risen partly for social reasons, urban life was proving less attractive to greater landlords, who began more and more to live in rural villas (see Plate X). Perforce the Empire shifted slowly toward more direct relations with the countryside to maintain its fundamental revenues of grain and other natural supplies, but here too "the argument from

X (*Continued*)

their prosperity; the villa itself has a bath suite with domed roofs.
Deutsches Archäologisches Institut

The great imperial villa near Piazza Armerina in Sicily was lavishly
decorated with mosaic floors. Above is a hunting scene, a very popular
sport of aristocrats in the Late Empire.

prosperity—or rather the decline of prosperity—is the same both
for the villages and the cities," as one prefect of Egypt commented.[19]

These significant changes in the countryside, alas, are not as
directly illuminated as one might wish. Throughout much of the
rural landscape ownership was concentrated in the hands of the
emperors themselves through their *patrimonium* and *res privata*,
but also the aristocracy held considerable and indeed growing

estates not only in Italy but throughout the provinces. The dues of imperial estates were collected by a system of procurators; aristocratic properties paid their taxes apparently through the local units of government. As fiscal pressure was applied to the cities and transmitted to the countryside, great landowners were able to cushion, though not entirely to escape, the demands; smaller landholders were in a weaker position and turned toward their more powerful neighbors for support, a process which seems at times to have turned them into tenant *coloni*. Legislation, as far as it existed in the chaos of the century, seems to have favored this process rather than banning it. Rural organization, in short, was undergoing a process of alteration which continued in the fourth century and produced almost autonomous rural units grouped around the villas of aristocrats, on whom the Empire came more and more to rest.

In the effort to create a tidy picture where chaos appears to reign the historian always runs the danger of undue simplification. In the preceding paragraphs I have sketched developments in the cities and countryside, the lines of which show only across the third and fourth centuries as a whole, for the processes at work were long protracted and are not subject to precise dating. Changes took place at different times in different places and not always in the same fashion. To consider only the cities, those on the Mediterranean Sea and especially the eastern urban centers continued to have an innate vigor which surfaced again in the fourth century. The unfortunate experiences of Gallic cities as they shrank into huddled, small communities within restricted walls have far too often been taken as a paradigm, for Gaul, after all, had been heavily subject to barbarian invasions in the third century.

Everywhere, however, the pressures of state, demands of declining production, of security of life, of invasions and wars brought more brutal ways of life and public punishments, in which the upper and lower classes were firmly distinguished in law. All the inhabitants of the Empire might now be citizens, but even in the first century after Christ a prefect of Egypt had pointed out, with regard to military citizenship, that "your status is not the same in each case. I have instructed the presidents of the nomes

to protect your privileges according to your particular condition."
A hidden tendency in the earlier centuries toward creating a police state also comes more into evidence in the third century in
desperate efforts to check disorder. Rural detachments under
beneficiarii were more common; Tertullian noted that in cities
there were official files of "shopkeepers, butchers, thieves, gam-
blers, and pimps" as well as of Christians.[20] Not only in the countryside but also in the cities the state officially bound *curiales,*
long-distance shippers of grain, bakers, and other essential personnel to their tasks. It is perhaps too much to say that the Roman Empire was freezing its structure to prevent alteration,
which could only be deleterious; but the metaphor is a useful one
to which we shall return in the next chapter.

The Reorganization by Diocletian and Constantine

A gold coin of Diocletian struck at Siscia about 286 may be taken
as an interesting specific illumination, both consciously and unconsciously, of the place of this great ruler, perhaps rightly called
a second Augustus (see Plate XI). On the obverse is a bust of
Diocletian in wreath and cuirass, befitting the militarization of
the Empire in the third century; this portrait and those of his co-
rulers "show the emperors as tough rulers—short-haired, strong-
jawed, and level-eyed—who survey their task without any hint of
personal feelings that lie short of duty."[21] The inscription starkly
reads "Imp Diocletianus P[ius] F[elix] Aug." No longer is there
emphasis on the title *pater patriae,* tribunician power, or other
ingredients of the Augustan constitution; the words pious and
fortunate, paraded regularly from Commodus on, refer rather to
a connection to divine favor, a concept stressed especially by
Gallienus, Aurelian, and their successors.

On the reverse is a nude male figure with staff and lightning
bolt labelled *Iovi conservatori,* Jupiter the Preserver. This figure
appears on Roman coinage first as a heartfelt concept during the
civil wars of 68–69, on issues struck in Gaul. Thereafter it turns
up periodically, often with the word "Augustus," to suggest that
Jupiter was supporting the emperor, on whose shoulders rested
the safety of the state; here the emphasis is certainly on Diocle-

XI Late Roman Rulers. On this gold coin (enlarged three times) Diocletian is dressed in wreath and cuirass; the reverse depicts Jupiter the Preserver (Christian hatred of the last imperial persecutor saw to it that virtually no busts of Diocletian survive).

The last great emperor of the fourth century was Valentinian I, whose powerful majesty is probably shown in this bronze statue from Barletta in southern Italy (looted from Constantinople in 1204). *Above, Hess/Leu Auktion 24 (1964), no. 347; below,* Brunn-Bruckmann, *Griechische und römische Porträts 896* tian's restoration of the Roman state religion and his own position as "Jovius," likewise under the protection of its greatest deity. Both the ruthlessly simplified bust and the figure of Jupiter reflect the artistic mutation which we noted earlier in this chapter.

Only through such numismatic evidence, inscriptions (such as the famous Price Edict), legal pronouncements, and scant historical references can we appreciate the many-sided activities of Diocletian; for he launched the only really Empire-wide and protracted persecution of the Christians and in consequence suffered damnation of his memory. As between Diocletian and Constantine it is often difficult to determine responsibility for the major reforms which produced the Later Roman Empire. On the whole Diocletian, who was much better educated and more flexible, probably had the main hand in shaping the civil administration; military reorganization, on the other side, owed much to Constantine, a son of war, who was brutal and dictatorial in his actions.

In an effort to halt the imperial merry-go-round of the third century Diocletian thus engaged in the most calculated and thoughtful effort to regularize succession which was tried in imperial history. He appointed as co-emperor the able general Maximian in 286 to control the western provinces and restore their frontiers; soon thereafter each Augustus received an aide, a Caesar. In 305 Diocletian forced his co-emperor to join in formal abdication—the only examples in all imperial history until the last emperor in the west—and the Caesars, Constantius and Galerius, moved up to be Augusti, two new Caesars being appointed. The scheme was neat but ineffective, for the dynastic principle still was potent. Maximian had a son Maxentius who seized power in Italy; Constantius also had a son, Constantine, who was elevated to the purple at York in 306 on his father's death. After a new series of civil wars Constantine became master of the whole Empire by 324 and in his turn founded a dynasty which lasted on to 363.

Many of Diocletian's other reforms were more successful. The provinces were broken up into some 96 small units, now including Italy, which were grouped on the civil side into 12 dioceses under vicars and these in turn into 4 prefectures; by this time one can perhaps truly speak of an imperial bureaucracy, largely cloaked in military form, for which we even have a handbook, *Notitia Dignitatum* (list of offices). Under this bureaucracy lay a great range of state factories of arms, textiles, etc. On the military side, clearly separated from civil administration, local *duces* commanded frontier garrisons, which were supported by a considerable amount of construction of forts (especially from Constantine onward); central reserves were under Masters of the Soldiers (*magistri militum*), ready to march on the somewhat restored road network to any threatened zone. Partly as a consequence of this double military structure the armed forces rose to the neighborhood of 500,000 men, a terrific burden in manpower and expense. Diocletian himself was not a spectacular general, but his aides Maximian in the west and the eastern Caesar Galerius brought renewed security to all the frontiers.

Diocletian also consolidated the fiscal changes and experiments of the third century. An empire-wide census was carried out which measured all productive forces in units called in many parts of the Empire the *iugum* (of land) and *caput* (of human beings and animals), though their precise definitions are not easily made. It is commonly assumed that the payment of the land tax (*iugatio*) in kind represented a great change from the Early Empire, but as observed at several points in earlier chapters we really do not know what proportion of the earlier *tributum solis* had been rendered in kind as against cash. The real advance in the Diocletianic system was that on the basis of these assessments the taxes could be fairly levied instead of resorting to the arbitrary and spasmodic depredation of the third century. As a prefect of Egypt announced,

> Our most provident Emperors . . . having learned that the levies of the public taxes were being made capriciously . . . decided in the interest of their provincials to root out this most evil and ruinous practice and to issue a salutary rule to which the taxes would have to conform.[22]

Other taxes in coin and gold were levied on industry and trade and the senators. Diocletian also conducted in 294 a thorough reform of the coinage, issuing from 14 mints gold, silver, and bronze coins; as retariffed by Constantine the gold *solidus* was to remain unchanged for the next 700 years.

Diocletian tried to check the inflation of preceding decades by his Edict of Maximum Prices in 301, though this had, as one might expect, only limited success. In many other aspects of imperial life Diocletian was equally thorough in a conservative fashion. At what date peasants became tied to their land virtually as serfs we do not know, but certainly by the time of Constantine and probably even Diocletian they were attached so firmly to the tax register of their estate or village that movement was impossible.

The imperial position itself had become steadily more "sacred" and removed from the common folk save on festival days; now all who gained an audience had to kneel and kiss the hem of his purple robe on entry and departure—the masters of the Roman world were no longer "saluted" on reception but "adored." Both to enhance the ruler's dignity and to safeguard his life approach was made more difficult and court ceremonial greater. On the other hand "the emperor, who is shut up in his palace, cannot know the truth," and could only rely on his councillors to tell him what actually was happening in his realm.[23] Diocletian continued the program of the later third-century rulers to reduce the place of the senatorial aristocracy as against that of the imperial bureaucracy; but by the time of Constantine the highest levels of the aristocracy were once again in a powerful political position as the equestrian and senatorial orders fused into one leading class.

The Empire must be protected by the gods of state, and to this end the ruler must enforce religious obedience. Diocletian fiercely banned the alien Manichean cult, which had gained considerable support in the east, and even addressed himself forcefully to the problem of Christianity, a network of churches spread all over the Empire which was stubbornly independent of imperial authority, but here he failed. His eventual successor Constantine, a deeply superstitious man, came in dream to believe the Christian God was on his side, a belief reenforced by military and political success; and when Constantine proceeded to found a new eastern capital from which the Empire could control both Balkan and eastern frontier defenses he fashioned Constantinople as a Christian city.

In the reign of Augustus, as Tacitus put it, the Roman state gained peace and the *princeps,* i.e., it gave up political freedom for internal and external security. Now men yielded economic and social freedom for renewed order and a *dominus* or lord, though Constantine was the first to use this title officially or to wear a diadem. After the whirlwinds of the third century had thus been tamed, the major supports of imperial unity which we have considered in preceding chapters still stood, even if one may suspect that their strength had been weakened. One, indeed—the urban centers—had deteriorated markedly in the west, though more by necessity than by choice. In partial compensation a new buttress was added by Constantine when he wholeheartedly embraced Christianity and made it a legal cult, though as we shall observe in the next chapter its support was to be markedly different in the eastern and western provinces.

Above all the leading classes still adhered to the Empire. Vocally their loyalty was paraded in a series of Latin panegyrics delivered before Augusti and Caesars across the fourth century; it has also been detected in a rambling collection of prophecies called the Sibylline Oracles.[24] Perhaps even more impressive testimony is the fact that the last ruler of the Imperium Galliarum deserted his troops in battle and accepted Aurelian as the true leader of the Roman world; in the east Aurelian had somewhat more difficulty in dealing with the Palmyrene kingdom, but the eastern provinces themselves came back easily to obedience. Modern scholars have at times made much of the revival in the third century of local religious cults, artistic styles, and languages; but these, to repeat an earlier warning, have little to do with the fundamental quality of Romanization in the sense of identification with the Empire. Whether this loyalty would continue in the next century might be problematical, but it had withstood the first test of the third century; and the reforms of Diocletian and Constantine gave the Empire a breathing spell.

Notes

1. *Digest,* 1. 4. 1.
2. Sherwin-White, *Roman Citizenship,* pp. 279–87, 380–94, and *Journal of Roman Studies,* 63 (1972), pp. 86–98; Dio Cassius 77. 15.
3. Grant, *The Climax of Rome,* p. xvi.
4. E. H. Swift, *Roman Sources of Christian Art* (New York, 1951), p. 198.
5. H. P. L'Orange, *Apotheosis in Ancient Portraiture* (Oslo, 1947), p. 111.
6. Tacitus, *Annals* 4. 32.
7. Tacitus, *Germany* 37.
8. Owen Lattimore, *Inner Asian Frontiers of China* (New York, 1940).
9. Gregory, *Epistola canonica* 1 (J. P. Migne, *Patrologia graeca,* 10 [Paris, 1857], col. 1021).
10. Luttwak, *Grand Strategy,* p. 175.
11. Mathias Hougen, parliamentary commissioner for the Reichswehr, as quoted in *Economist,* March 14, 1970, p. 41.
12. Cf. MacMullen, *Response to Crisis,* p. 33 on *restitutor.*
13. Cyprian, *To Demetrianus* 3–11.
14. *L'Année épigraphique* 1931, no. 38.
15. W. L. Westermann and A. A. Schiller, *Apokrimata* (New York, 1950), lines 40–44, an order repeated in *Theodosian Code* 7. 41. 1; *Select Papyri,* ed. A. S. Hunt and C. C. Edgar, 2 (London, 1934), no. 230 (A.D. 260).
16. Callu, *ANRW,* 2. 2, p. 604.
17. J. K. Galbraith, *The Affluent Society* (Boston, 1958), pp. 265–66.
18. R. Yohanen, quoted by D. Sperber, *Antiquité classique,* 38 (1969), p. 167.
19. T. C. Skeat and E. P. Wegener, *Journal of Egyptian Archaeology,* 21 (1953), pp. 224–47 (*c.* A.D. 250).
20. *Fontes iuris romani anteiustiniani,* ed. V. Arangio-Ruiz, 3 (Florence, 1943), no. 171 (A.D. 63); Tertullian, *On Flight in Persecution* 13 (*Corpus Christianorum,* series Latina 2 [1954]).
21. C. H. V. Sutherland, *Roman Imperial Coinage,* 6 (London, 1967), p. 109.
22. *The Archive of Aurelius Isidorus,* ed. A. E. R. Boak and H. C. Youtie (Ann Arbor, 1960), p. 29 (A.D. 297).
23. A. Alföldi, *Die monarchische Repräsentation im römischen Kaiserreiche* (Darmstadt, 1977), p. 39; *SHA Aurelian* 43.
24. Sherwin-White, *Roman Citizenship,* pp. 445–57.

CHAPTER VIII

The Final Test (*A.D. 330-476*)

After the death of Constantine members of his family held imperial power through the brief reign of the pagan Julian (360–63). Thereafter Valentinian, often considered the last great emperor, protected the western parts of the Empire (see Plate XI), and his brother Valens the eastern half until his death in the disastrous defeat by the Goths at Adrianople (378). To restore order Valentinian appointed Theodosius in the east, who eventually became ruler of a reunited Empire, only to divide it between his sons Arcadius in the east and Honorius in the west. After 395 the Empire was never again under the control of one Caesar.

As reconstituted by Diocletian and Constantine the realm enjoyed a new burst of prosperity in which its leading elements displayed their wealth through a remarkable wave of building. Constantinople was created as a virtually new metropolis, though embellished with ancient works of art from all Greece. Trier was adorned with buildings some of which still stand; Milan, the western capitol through most of the fourth century—"Rome is where the emperor may be," as a third-century historian put it[1]—received its due attention until Honorius retreated to the more secure fortress of Ravenna behind its marshes. Rome might well be thought to have had enough imperial building in earlier centuries, and indeed after the Severi saw very little construction beyond Aurelian's wall; but in the fourth century it experienced an architectural explosion. Diocletian erected a huge set of baths, parts of which now house a major museum and also a church (see Plate XII); we have already inspected the Basilica and Arch of Constantine; and now the bishops of Rome built basilican

XII Baths of Diocletian. The Late Empire still had great resources at the command of its emperors; this reconstruction of the Baths of Diocletian in Rome suggests how large and magnificent were its vaulted halls. E. Paulin, *Thermes de Dioclétien*

churches in which numbers of the faithful could gather for mass— St. Peter's, San Giovanni in Laterano, San Paolo fuori le mure, and on into the fifth century with Santa Maria Maggiore, Santa Maria in Trastevere, and other churches. Even in the countryside imperial hunting lodges such as Piazza Armerina in Sicily as well as aristocratic villas flourished (see Plate X).

Christianity throve mightily under imperial approval and support, and was fortunate in having a relatively tranquil century in which to improve its organization enough to ride out the following storms and to thrash out critical doctrinal disputes in debates the intellectual vigor of which was almost incredibly different from the sterile classical rhetoric of the pagan world. What is good for one part of society, however, is not always good for all. The church voraciously swallowed both money and men, and perhaps the men could be less easily spared. That is, Ambrose had been governor of Milan when its populace demanded him as bishop; Augustine was well launched on a rhetorical career when he was converted to Christianity and returned to

Africa to become bishop of Hippo; Jerome could have had a public career rather than becoming the scholar of Bethlehem. After Paulinus of Nola sold off his family's wealth and became an ascetic, even Ambrose commented, "What will our leading citizens say when they hear this? It is unthinkable that a man of such family, such background, such genius, gifted with such eloquence, should retire from the Senate and that the succession of so noble a family should be broken."[2] Many men of ability, in other words, turned away from public service, partly no doubt because they could have a freer hand in church offices than in the bureaucracy, but also out of concern for their own souls and those of their fellow men; others made a fuller retreat from the world in joining the growing monastic movement.

The volume and variety of literary evidence for the fourth century is almost staggering. Not since the last century of the Republic can we listen so fully to protagonists speaking for themselves: in the church, from Eusebius under Constantine on to Augustine in the early fifth century; in political life, the emperor Julian as well as other rulers through their legislation; in cultural circles, Claudian the poet, Libanius and Themistius the orators, and Ammianus Marcellinus, the last great historian of antiquity. Particularly in pagan writers there was extensive attention to the past; scholars engaged in an almost desperate effort to copy manuscripts and write commentaries on the works of Virgil, summations of Roman history, or treatises on Roman institutions. If we were surveying imperial history in a chronological manner we should have to give far more attention to the fourth and fifth centuries than will be feasible, for the new frame of culture which emerged in the third century led to remarkable achievements. My main objective here, however, is to consider the dissolution of the supports for imperial order, especially in the western provinces.

Freezing—and Unfreezing

Politically the structure of the Later Roman Empire is one of the grimmest of all ancient times. In theory emperors were chosen by God, the Senate, and the army, and in inscriptions are often hailed as "born for the good of the state"; but once in office they were sacred *domini,* "our autocratic despots over earth and sea and all races of men."[3] Curtains and masses of courtiers separated them from the subjects; in public the rulers appeared almost as automata, stiff in robes and protocol, as pictured by Ammianus Marcellinus on Constantius' visit to Rome. Within their palaces, which now at last had eunuchs, they gave formal audiences only to foreign ambassadors and important subjects; for advice they relied on a *consistorium,* consisting not of the freely chosen "friends" of unofficial standing in the Early Empire but mainly of executive officials. These in turn supervised an intricately ordered bureaucracy, divided into military and civil sections, numbering by the fifth century some 30,000, which reached into the urban levels. From the praetorian prefects downward all "were inflamed with a boundless eagerness for riches, without consideration for justice or right," or as other writers put it bureaucrats sold "smoke," i.e., promise of assistance with the machinery of government which was not given in reality—heaping up their piles of gold while the Empire in the west went to pieces. Direct personal appeals to the ruler were no longer favored; "the means of petition" Diocletian announced, "were not to be granted to everyone unreservedly and indiscriminately."[4]

Since change meant decay, the Empire was resolved to stop change. The Theodosian Code, a collection of fourth-century edicts in the main, contains provision after provision by which the state sought to lock men of all trades and services in their places and to secure from every subject his due contribution to the coffers and granaries of the Empire. "No man," said one edict to the people, "shall possess any property that is tax exempt."[5] Apparently taxes doubled across the fourth century to support the swollen army of up to half a million men and administrative staffs, this in a period of stagnant or declining production; and runaway inflation occurred again from Constantine onward. To modern eyes the corrupt, brutal regimentation of the Later Empire appears as a horrible example of the victory of the state over the individual, and the fact that the rulers arrived at this situation in their efforts to maintain the framework of ancient civilization is the most rueful of irony.

The more the Empire tottered, the more evident became repression and terrorism. The concept of lèse-majesté remained a potent tool to strike down opponents; any man of importance might dream in times of stress "of the torturer and of fetters and lodgings of darkness."[6] Astrology, magic, and poisoning were directed against the rulers or against fellow nobles on a scale unprecedented in earlier ages, and the discovery of their employment led to fearful repression by such emperors as Valens. Many a political and social law began with rhetorical praises of the ruler's mercy and serenity and then ordained the most frightful of punishments—maiming of legs, gouging of eyes, burning alive— for violations of its provisions. Nor was it solely the government which exhibited barbaric brutality. The sophist Libanius, a proud partisan of ancient culture, believed in the crudest of magic and exulted at a famine in the city where his son died; Egyptian papyri attest that in the Nile Valley men with official influence could physically assault the weak with impunity.

In the countryside the Empire had essentially to surrender the humanitarian rules of earlier centuries and give control of the peasants to the landlords, a development to which we shall return; in the cities the town councillors or *curiales* were firmly and fiercely tied to their posts in order that imperial revenues might be garnered in case of deficiencies—they themselves for a time were fully responsible though this provision had lapsed by the end of the fourth century. If they failed in their duties they might even be whipped; Libanius bitterly reports, "In many a city, your majesty, after these floggings this is what the few surviving councillors say: 'Goodby house, goodbye lands! Let the one and the other be sold, and with their price let us buy liberty'."[7]

Yet the repeated edicts of the Theodosian Code banning movement and change suggest in their very repetition that the realities of the fourth century may have been very much otherwise. In fact there had never been as much physical or social mobility and structural change. Perforce thousands upon thousands had had earlier to flee barbarian invasions and were again on the roads of the Empire before the end of the fourth century; barbaric tribes were permitted to enter the Empire, as the Goths in 376, so that the frontiers no longer sharply distinguished the civilized from the uncivilized. Service in the imperial bureaucracy could lead men of modest origins to the highest civil and military posts, no longer the exclusive preserve of equestrian and senatorial aristocrats; by the end of the century almost all the great generals such as Stilicho had Germanic names.

West and East

Down to 395 the Later Empire still appeared solid, but 11 years later a complete breakdown of the Rhenish frontier meant that the western Empire was doomed even if its deathbed agony was as long as the last act of *Tristan und Isolde*. Yet this disaster affected only the west; the eastern Empire remained unified, and was to continue for many centuries thereafter.

The present study is not primarily intended as an investigation of the causes of the Decline and Fall, which have been endlessly discussed since the Renaissance; nowhere can one better see how modern concerns alter our view of the past—"for all times co-exist, and the future can sometimes affect the past, even though the past is a road that leads to the future."[8] Any explanation must be a wide-ranging exploration of psychological, spiritual, and even transcendental attitudes as well as more mundane attentions. My main concern throughout the preceding chapters has been rather to explore the forces and institutions which supported so magnificently the survival of the Empire for centuries; but now, in the western provinces, these proved at last inadequate to withstand the stresses of internal decay and external invasion. The cities declined or disappeared, the aristocracy became independent of the imperial administration, and the Christian church adopted a very ambivalent attitude toward the state. After examining these changes we may then briefly inspect the political and military deterioration which produced the Decline and Fall itself.

Two vital characteristics of the Empire were noted in earlier pages but need always to be kept in mind. At least 65 per cent of imperial revenues came from the eastern provinces, but two thirds of the army was stationed on the western frontiers. When the Empire underwent permanent division in 395, the result was a terrific, indeed insoluble fiscal problem for western administrators. To give only one example at this point, relating to the old Roman custom of reenforcing diplomacy by bribes, Stilicho found it impossible to raise enough funds from imperial resources or Roman aristocrats to satisfy the Visigothic leader Alaric, who proceeded to take Rome in 410 and sack it for three days.

The division of the Empire itself was not the accidental result of the fact that Theodosius had two sons. As far back as the joint reigns of Marcus Aurelius and Lucius Verus the Empire had needed generals and administrators with imperial power on at least two fronts; it was suggested that Caracalla and his brother Geta thus divide the Empire, and across the third and fourth centuries joint rulers had appeared at many points. The separation, however, went deeper. By the fourth century men of letters in the west were less and less likely to know Greek—Augustine, for example, was almost entirely Greekless—and especially in the church one can detect a sense that east and west were distinct. Basil of Cappadocia broke out in a letter concerning pope Damasus, "If the anger of God persists, what aid can the pride of the West bring us?" while in the west Ambrose repeats the opinion of Italian bishops, "We are often blamed for not seeming to value highly unison with the Eastern brethren, and for seeming to refuse their good will." Both authors comment specifically on the difficulties of travel especially by land and even of communication: "Formerly it was the glory of the church that from one end of earth to the other brothers coming from each individual church, equipped with little tokens of identity as with provisions for the trip, could find everywhere fathers and brothers . . . [now] we have shut ourselves up in separate cities, and each of us suspects his neighbor."[9]

After the final political and military division eastern emperors continued to try to shore up their weaker western brothers by occasional provision of money, troops, and even the appointment of the emperors Anthemius, Olybrius, and Nepos when no western authority could do so. If Attila the Hun failed to attack Rome in 452 it was not primarily because Roman civil leaders and pope Leo had traveled north to beg his mercy but rather because the eastern emperor Marcian had sent an expedition under

Aetius (not the famous western patrician) to invade the Hunnish homeland and threaten his control over neighboring German tribes. But such sporadic aid was not to be enough.

The decline of the cities and the rising power of aristocrats seems to have been far more pronounced in the western provinces than in the east. There is little archeological evidence for villas in the east; though patronage played a considerable part in Syria to judge from Libanius' oration on the subject villagers continued to be landowners and to lie more directly under imperial control and protection. Both in east and west imperial pressure was heavy on the cities, but whereas in the west local machinery of government was virtually replaced by imperial officials in the fifth century the town councils of the east continued to have a significant role. Cities such as Constantinople, Ephesus, and Antioch persisted in some degree of prosperity and were still attractive to men of wealth and culture, who reenforced the urban councils; John Chrysostom incidentally observed that men "can stay at ease in well-fortified cities. If wars come they are outside or at the bounds of Roman rule—as in the land of the Tigris or in British islands." Across the fourth century the emperors had sought to protect the poor in the cities by providing a "defender of the city" (*defensor civitatis* or *plebis*), but in the west by the early fifth century this official was chosen by the bishop, military commander, and rural magnates along with the *curiales* and undoubtedly came to represent their interests. Only in the west did the emperors have to issue edicts trying to ban flight of *curiales* and artisans from the towns to the countryside where "great men" could protect them; one such decree sadly noted, "The cities have lost the splendor in which they once shone."[10]

As far as cities and long-range commerce are concerned, generalizations are dangerous. The evidence from known shipwrecks suggests a marked decline in overseas trade in the third and fourth centuries, and the difficulties in communications attested by ecclesiastical comments may reenforce a subjective view that commerce declined. Yet though security on the seas was even less certain after the Vandals took Africa, in 429 and following years trade did continue to some degree. On land the roads were no longer well maintained, but pilgrimages from Bordeaux to Jerusalem could still take place. When the walled perimeter of Autun was reduced from 5 kilometers to 1.3, it is evident that this center was no longer a city but simply a fortress under the control of a chieftain, which now no longer had the secure water supplies of an aqueduct. In southern Gaul and Italy, on the other hand, urban life had not yet disappeared, if indeed it ever did. A cautious but reasonable conclusion would be that the western Empire could not depend as well as could the east on local units of government for maintenance of order or the supply of revenues in cash.

The decisive alterations, however, in the west were connected with its aristocracy, which we can see best in Rome and Gaul. Long, long ago the aristocrats of Rome itself had been masters of the Roman Republic, but then they had been fettered by Augustus and became ever more "house-broken" as emperor succeeded emperor until their retirement, forced and optional, from public life in the later third century. Now the wheels of history turned again, and the aristocrats became ever more liberated in the later fourth and fifth centuries. The emperors of the west were to disappear, but not the aristocracy.

In the ancestral center, the city of Rome, aristocrats still vied to be prefect of the city or to enjoy the honor of the consulship, and others served as praetorian prefect over Italy; but in court offices proper aristocrats came back into prominence only to some degree in the troubled fifth century, and on the whole the aristocracy was ever more disjoined from western imperial administration. Ammianus Marcellinus bitterly portrays the aristocrats of his day as leading lives of idle luxury and ostentation in Rome.

In passing he comments on their exaggerations of their wealth, "doubling the annual yields of their fields, well cultivated (as they think) of which they assert that they possess a great number from the rising to the setting sun."[11] But in truth the landed wealth of the greatest aristocrats is almost unimaginable, especially when set beside the general decline of the cities. Melania the Younger, for example, owned lands in Italy, Sicily, Africa, Spain, and Gaul, the revenues of which have been calculated to have been as much as the taxes of two African provinces; when she adopted the life of a true Christian after the sack of Rome by Alaric, she freed 8000 slaves who wished to be liberated and sold the others to her brother. In her retirement Melania lived simply with only 15 eunuchs and 60 maidens! Aristocrats such as Ausonius and Sidonius Apollinaris in Gaul and others in Africa came to abandon the cramped, melancholy towns huddling behind walls and dwelt at least during summers in their villas, foreshadowing the life of medieval nobles. They were, in fine, being liberated from intimate association with the cities.

The rise of large agricultural units, independent of the cities and to a considerable degree free in practice from state control, was an important economic development of the Later Empire in the west, foreshadowings of which we examined in the preceding chapter. At that time parts of the imperial landed estates moved into aggressive private hands which could better keep the land in cultivation; this process continued in the fourth century by imperial gifts or perpetual leases and sales. When oppressed by imperial bailiffs peasants at time threatened to flee from the imperial estates to private protectors; in other areas, where peasants had previously owned their own lands, they turned to the patronage (*patrocinium*) of local magnates for economic support, mediation in disputes, or protection against the imperial soldiery and barbarian invaders. Although independent small landholders did not entirely disappear, the typical form of rural organization changed ever more into a self-sufficient agricultural complex dependent socially, economically, and even politically on a lord; art and crafts tended to migrate from the cities to these rural centers.

Theoretically the writ of the emperor still ran in estates and cities alike, and the emperors sought to stem the currents of dissolution by asserting their sacred position in edicts and by supporting the urban machinery. It was the master of the villa or country estate, however, who furnished imperial recruits and paid imperial taxes, but now was no longer under the ostensible control of the local units of government; such dues as he felt it wise to pay went straight to the provincial administration. Insofar as the rural territory of a *civitas* or *polis* thus became independent, the strength of the urban machinery was further weakened. Accompanying this rise of rural manors was the decline in the population of the Empire, the dimensions of which cannot be statistically measured though it appears that by the fifth century one third of the farmlands in Africa Proconsularis and nearly 10 per cent in Asia lay deserted and thus no longer paid their regular dues to the cities.[12]

Sometimes the incipient serfs refused to accept their lot calmly. The countryside of Africa was harassed by wandering bands who adopted the cloak of the Donatist heresy; in Gaul and Spain similar unrest was known; in the fifth century the peasants were at times to turn in relief to the invading barbarians, who might free them from the terrific social and economic pressures of the decaying imperial and urban systems. A fugitive Greek among the Huns agreed that "the laws and constitutions of the Romans were fair" but deplored the ruthless exaction of taxes, and the unprincipled, unchecked conduct of the well-to-do. To him life with Huns was far better.[13]

Not always, though, did the peasants object to the changes, which gained for themselves and their descendants an inseparable tie with a piece of land from which their master could exact only those dues fixed by law or by custom of the estate. Any assessment of the "statism" of the Later Empire must include the fact that the orders of the rulers, though more destructive of individual freedom of movement and action, bore directly on a far smaller proportion of the population than had the edicts of such a ruler as Trajan. Beneath the surface the aristocrats and the peasants were fashioning a network of stable, independent cells which would survive the withering away of the western Empire and the disappearance of a money economy.

Another framework of social and religious order also would survive in the form of the Christian churches. Although Eusebius could trill under Constantine, "Two roots of blessing, the Roman Empire and the doctrine of Christian piety, sprang up together for the benefit of man," the Christian church was not inclined to yield totally its earlier independence of the state,[14] and here too developments in the west took a very different course from those in the east. Eastern bishops tended to bend before the emperor and his bureaucracy, and those who did not were likely to suffer; John Chrysostom died in exile after twice being banished from his see of Constantinople. Western ecclesiastical leaders maintained a stiffer attitude. It was Ambrose of Milan who humbled Theodosius after a bloody massacre of the unruly residents of Thessalonica in 390 and forced him to open penance; in matters of faith he declared, "The bishops are wont to judge Christian emperors, not emperors the bishops." Even more direct was Lucifer, bishop of Cagliari, who in exile wrote five open attacks on the emperor Constantius, threatening him with divine judgment for his support of the Arian heresy and abusing him as "the filth of the sewers," "founder of blasphemy," and so on.[15]

The attitude of the western church toward German invaders was perhaps as a result an ambivalent one. The sad fact that those Germans who were already Christianized were Arians caused theological troubles; but in practical terms bishops, as protectors of their flocks, often sought accommodation with the barbarians. In saints' lives it is bishops and monks, not civil or military leaders, who secured the release of captives and otherwise treated with the invaders. Pope Leo, as already noted, sought to dissuade Attila from invading Italy and secured from Gaiseric the agreement that in plundering Rome in 455 the Vandals would not rape or assault the Roman populace. In return the Germans appear to have been respectful toward local ecclesiastical authorities; in the sack of Rome by Alaric the Gothic leader ordered restoration of sacred vessels which were solemnly paraded to St. Peter's.

In commenting on the increase of barbarian pressures Ambrose warned that internal enemies—cupidity, temptation—were more serious threats than external dangers, and in this judgment he was certainly correct. The priest Salvian, writing in southern Gaul *c.* 445, goes far toward explaining the collapse of western imperial authority in a bitter remark which applies more to the class of *curiales* than to the great aristocrats, "In the districts taken over by the barbarians there is one desire among all the Romans, that they should never again find it necessary to pass under Roman jurisdiction."[16] As one surveys the dismal series of emperors and generals in the fifth century it is clear that the western Empire was simply eroding at an ever-accelerating pace.

Little by little, thus, the western emperors simply abdicated authority or responsibility for outlying districts. Pannonia seems to have been evacuated by the time of Alaric's march through it, and thereby major routes of communication between the Danube and the east were yielded. The upper classes of the Balkans eventually retreated to more secure districts; so too aristocrats in Gaul moved south of the Loire by the middle of the fifth century as northern Gaul fell under the power of the Franks. After the death of Saint Severinus, who protected by firmness and piety the Romans of Noricum from famine and barbarian threats, local leaders stuck it out only another six years and then moved down into Italy, carrying with them the remains of their saint on an oxcart; eventually these relics came to rest near Naples in a monastery created out of the Lucullan villa to which Romulus Augustulus, the last western Emperor, had been sent. In 407 Alaric invited Honorius to hand over Noricum officially since it was scarcely paying any taxes; three years later Roman rule in Britain ended, as we shall see in greater detail later.

Dissolution of the Western Empire

Two main supports of imperial unity, the central administration and the local units of government, were declining on their own; but it is also true that the degree of external pressure on western frontiers was far more severe than in the east, where the Empire was at war with Sassanian Persia for only 40 years between 284 and 524. Valentinian had done his best to improve a static line of defense on the Rhine, judging that "it was a more valuable service to check the barbarians by frontier defenses than to defeat them in battle."[17] The last successful Roman sally across the Rhine took place in 393. But in the winter of 406 the whole Danubian and Rhenish frontiers collapsed as up to 200,000 Sueves, Vandals, Alans, and others swept across Gaul and into Spain. When the local landlords and peasants of northern Spain tried to bar the Pyrenees its passes were opened to the Sueves by a "Roman" military unit.

Stilicho wiped out the group which entered Italy, but elsewhere the best the Empire could do was to make accommodations with the invaders by allowing them to occupy and rule wide tracts of Gaul and Spain, though in doing so the imperial administration used the Visigoths, already settled in Gaul, to keep the new entrants from the Mediterranean coasts and formally banned the training of barbarians in ship-handling. Nonetheless Gaiseric led his Vandals across the straits of Gibraltar in 429 and wrested control of all north Africa and then Sicily; in 442 the Empire formally recognized his practical independence. By then the Huns, a mobile cavalry, had succeeded the Germans as the threat to the Empire.

Throughout the later fourth century the western Empire had been far more beset by challenges to the throne than was the east; in the fifth, effective organization against external threats was made difficult by dissensions between rulers and their military commanders which so weakened the imperial position as to render its holders almost puppets. The suspicious emperor Honorius had Stilicho murdered in 408, which removed the most useful bar to Visigothic pressure. Constantius, as patrician from 413 (a title now denoting generalissimo), managed to settle the Visigoths in southwest France, as just noted, and became emperor himself in 421, but died before the year was out. Thereafter the son of Constantius and Galla Placidia, Valentinian III, became emperor at the age of 6 and ruled 30 years. For most of this period he was "supported" by the patrician Aetius, who destroyed the Burgundian kingdom (reflected in the *Nibelungenlied*), thereafter combined with the Visigoths to defeat Attila and the Huns in the battle of the Catalaunian Plains in 451, but in turn was murdered in 454.

By this time it is very difficult to visualize what constituted a "Roman army." Drafting of sons of soldiers had come to a close by the end of the fourth century; two desperate edicts of 406 urged even slaves to enlist as well as "all men who are aroused by the innate spirit of freedom," but lest this not be enough 10 gold solidi were promised (3 down and the rest "when matters have been adjusted").[18] But by mid-century the troops under Roman banners must have been largely "federate" bands of barbarians fighting for pay and no better disciplined or equipped than their foes. In turn it is not easy to see whence the imperial treasury by this time could derive funds, though coinage at least in gold did continue. As the author of a saint's life comments with regard to the Norican frontier, "While the Roman Empire still stood, soldiers were maintained with public pay in many towns for the defense of the frontier, but when that custom lapsed the military units were abolished along with the frontier." A delegation went from Noricum to seek its pay under Honorius, but on the way its members were killed by barbarians.[19] When troubles emerged in areas still technically under Roman rule, as in Hispania Tarraconensis menaced by the Sueves, the best course of events often was to invite another German tribe—in this case the Visigoths—to intervene.

After Valentinian III no emperor held the throne more than six years; finally in 476 the Germanic master of Italy, Odoacer, deposed the youthful puppet Romulus Augustulus, who lived on in Campania to the second decade of the sixth century, and sent the imperial regalia to Constantinople. In the west, to sum up, three vital supports for imperial unity—the position of the emperor, the central administration, and the army—had vanished; the cities were much weakened or destroyed; the aristocracy had greatly changed its way of life; Roman civilization survived, but in attentuated forms which were less and less connected with the Greek-speaking world. Three new bonds, however, had arisen to give structure to the incipient Middle Ages and to pass on some of the legacy of the ancient world. One was the union of Christians not as isolated individuals but bound together in the Body of Christ, superstitious and miracle-seeking but capable of producing bishops such as Gregory the Great at Rome or Caesarius at Arles who were forceful and cogent in their Latin letters, sermons, and tracts; in matters of doctrine, but not in direct jurisdiction, western ecclesiastical leaders usually deferred to the bishop of Rome. The second bond was the organization of the countryside in almost self-sufficient agricultural units, villages at times clustered by fortified manor houses of lords who remained reasonably well educated; where German invaders now dwelt they were settled in clumps distinct from the civil population. And thirdly the Germanic leaders themselves ruled formally constituted kingdoms which made considerable use of Roman law and even of administrative structures. Apart from the Sueves, who marauded ruthlessly in Spain until downed by the Visigoths, and to some extent the Vandals, who preyed on western naval commerce, the German invaders sought to conserve rather than destroy the society into which they had entered. This was especially true in areas where aristocrats had been well established, as in Gaul and above all in Italy; here the Ostrogothic kings employed aristocrats such as Boethius and Cassiodorus as administrators and secretaries and normally yielded outward deference to the Senate of Rome. This venerable body continued to exist on into the early seventh century.

But sometimes nothing survived the end of Roman rule.

The End of Roman Britain

In examining breakdowns in civilization a historian often will gain greater insight from looking not at the centers but at outlying fringes, where the civilized order is least well implanted. Thus in the collapse of the Bronze Age in the eastern Mediterranean at the close of the second millennium B.C., the Aegean world suffered most severely; the Mycenaean palaces with their advanced arts and the use of writing vanished, and Greece sank into semi-nomadic, almost unpopulated Dark Ages. Eventually, to be sure, order was restored, and the way had been paved by the earlier collapse for a new beginning, the root of Hellenic civilization.

With this parallel in mind let us consider the least-Romanized province in the west, Britain. Its conquest had been begun by Claudius in 43, who planned to occupy only the lowlands; but soon Roman generals found themselves forced to annex Wales and northern England as far as the region which became Hadrian's Wall. In the lowlands the trappings of Roman civilization soon appeared. Administrative centers were organized as cities, which at points developed a fair degree of trade and industry; Cirencester, it will be recalled, eventually had perhaps 20,000 inhabitants, though most *civitas*-capitals numbered only 2–5000. Villas of magnates emerged as focuses of agricultural production

to feed the cities (see Plate IV); across the third and fourth centuries these villas often came to sport impressive mosaic floors,
baths, and other refinements in keeping with the prosperity of
the cities, which flourished despite occasional difficulties with the
Picts from the North, Scots from Ireland, and Saxons from
Germany.

This adoption of Roman organization and culture was not
superficial, but it was not deeply rooted. Not a single native of
the island is known to have been a senator, and only one called
himself an equestrian. A recent collection of all Latin inscriptions
known from Roman Britain has 1298 items up to Hadrian's Wall,
a pitifully small group considering that a number are single letters and words. The bulk consists of tombstones and religious
dedications; there is not one major municipal decree or other
lengthy inscription, and even poetry appears only in three stones
from the vicinity of the wall.[20] Across the four centuries of Roman rule, one Briton played a part in Roman culture, the her-
etic Pelagius who upheld free will against Augustine's deter-
minism.

In the later fourth century two pretenders to the throne in
succession withdrew troops from Britain, which were not replaced. The last restoration of Hadrian's Wall was carried out
by British communities in 369; in the early fifth century some
forts on the wall may have continued to hold forgotten, useless
garrisons, but essentially the army had gone. Roman administrators soon followed the exodus. In 410 the council of British
civitates appealed to Honorius, who bluntly advised them to see
to their own protection; about 446 a further approach was made
to the patrician Aetius in vain. The only tie with the continent
of which we thereafter hear is a visit from Saint Germanus in 429
to settle the problem of Pelagianism; as an ex-*dux* of Armorica
Germanus led a militia in a victory over Saxons and Picts, and
may have returned again in 446–47. Thereafter descends "the
Tartarean blackness that engulfs late fifth-century Britain," a
darkness in which nonetheless a recent historian can see "the
lurid flames of burning cities and farmsteads . . . punctuated
from time to time by the screams and groaning of the dying

. . . the human pain which accompanied and followed the fall of the western Roman Empire is beyond even the figures of astronomy to calculate."[21]

The realities, as far as they can be guessed, are not quite so dramatic. It appears that leaders of the British countryside managed for some time to withstand the Saxons, thus giving the ultimate foundation for the beloved Arthurian tales of the Middle Ages and recent novelists; but by 600 Saxon kings controlled the English lowlands. Coinage had ceased to circulate about 430 as trade and imperial fiscal demands declined or disappeared. Legend suggests that the cities were ravaged by a plague in the 440s; exploration of the *civitas*-capitals yields inconclusive results but suggests their orderly occupation dissolved soon after 400 in reflection of the changes in economic and political patterns. As the cities disappeared so too did the villas, either through sack or more often simply by decay; agricultural units may occasionally have endured on into Saxon times. Cirencester became "an abandoned and virtually lifeless town" in which the dead were simply dumped in a roadside ditch, though the amphitheater may have continued to have had some population as in other Roman centers as far as Dacia.[22] Interestingly enough, however, the great legionary *principia* at York, in which Septimius Severus and Constantius Chlorus had died, was used by kings for several centuries; a monolithic column discovered a few years ago under York Cathedral suggests how impressive the building must have been.

Latin vanished completely from Saxon lands, though not from tombstones in North Britain and in Wales, where we even find a doctor and "citizen and magistrate."[23] The Christianized Celts of this area maintained some scant ties with the coast of Gaul and more direct connection with the growing monastic strength of Irish Christianity, but in the Saxon kingdoms the church also completely disappeared. In sum, the pillars on which the strength of the Roman Empire had depended—army, administration, aristocracy, urban organization, and eventually Christianity—were all gone; in Aethelbehrt's Kent Roman occupation had left no visible trace.

Conclusion

After existing half a millennium the Roman Empire, as constituted by Augustus and reorganized by Diocletian and Constantine, had proved to be the impossibility which I suggested in my introduction, at least in its western stretches. In two other studies of ancient history I have sought to show that the dissolution of the Empire in the west was a vital step in the development of medieval and modern European civilization; one cannot visualize how society could have directly progressed from the ruthless, violent autocracy of the Later Empire and its sterile culture, seeking only to preserve the past. Every now and then mankind must recoil and break its existing bonds before forging a new pattern of society.

The Roman Empire, however, was not the meaningless interlude suggested by events in Britain; nowhere else did all its inheritance disappear so completely. Even in England Christianity was to come back in the seventh century by way of Irish monks and the missionary activity of Augustine, sent from Rome in 597, and with it appeared again Latin, coinage, more formally organized states, and written laws. By the eighth century the first significant medieval historian, Bede, was active at Jarrow, and Charlemagne was soon to call on the Englishman Alcuin to head the palace school in the Frankish Empire. Did some hidden memories of a more advanced way of life linger far in the Saxon "unconscious" or was the rapid change due solely to contemporary continental influence, represented by Bertha, a Merovingian princess who married Aethelbehrt and brought with her the bishop of Senlis?

But what of men who lived during the Empire itself? If we were to ask the Jews, the farmers lying along lines of communication, the oppressed *curiales* of the Later Empire, we are not likely to find that they thought the Empire gave justice; and to repeat yet again Augustine's powerful question, "Justice being taken away, then, what are kingdoms but great robberies?" Lawyers, administrators, aristocrats, the upper classes of the cities in the Early Empire would on the other hand have returned a very different answer. Overall the political, economic, and military structure of the Empire was one of the most successful in human history in giving centuries of stability and order.

Always the average man leads a life of quiet desperation, in Thoreau's words, but down to the last century of the Empire in the west that desperation was at least tempered by a sense of earthly security. If Augustus' spirit could have looked down the five centuries which followed his death he might well have felt that he had deserved to be "called the author of the best possible government, and of carrying with me when I die the hope that the foundations which I have laid for the State will remain unshaken." Few leaders have been so successful.

Notes

1. Herodian 1. 6. 5.
2. *Epistle* 58 (*c.* 395).
3. Alföldi, *Representation,* p. 212; G. Petzl and H. W. Pleket, *Zeitschrift für Papyrologie und Epigraphik,* 35 (1979), p. 282, a milestone from Lydia.
4. Ammianus Marcellinus 16. 8. 12 (beginning according to the historian with Constantius); Friedländer, *Roman Life and Manners,* 1, p. 44; *Codex Justinianus* 7. 62. 6.
5. *Theodosian Code* 13. 10. 8 (A.D. 383).
6. Ammianus Marcellinus 28. 1. 16.
7. Libanius, *Oration* 28. 42.
8. Susan Cooper, *The Dark Is Rising* (New York, 1973), p. 45.
9. Ambrose, *Epistles* 14, 15, 56; Basil, *Epistles* 191, 239.
10. John Chrysostom (J. P. Migne, *Patrologia graeca* 56 [Paris, 1859], col. 33); *Theodosian Code* 12. 1. 146, 12. 19. 1, 14. 7. 1.
11. Ammianus Marcellinus 14. 6. 10.
12 Jones, *Ancient Economy,* pp. 84–85.
13. *Fragmenta historicorum graecorum,* ed. C. Müller, 4 (Paris, 1885), p. 86.
14. *Panegyric of Constantine* 16; K. M. Setton, *Christian Attitude Towards the Emperor in the Fourth Century Especially as Shown in Addresses to the Emperor* (New York, 1941), p. 48.
15. Ambrose, *Epistles* 21. 4; Lucifer, *On Saint Athanasius* 2. 26, *On Not Agreeing with Heretics* 9 (*Corpus Scriptorum Ecclesiasticorum Latinorum* 14; Setton, *Christian Attitude,* p. 97).
16. *On the Governance of God* 5. 8.

17. Ammianus Marcellinus 29. 4. 1.

18. *Theodosian Code* 7. 13. 16–17.

19. Eugippius, *Life of Severinus* 20 (ed. R. Noll; Berlin, 1963).

20. R. G. Collingwood and R. P. Wright, *The Roman Inscriptions of Britain*, 1 (Oxford, 1965).

21. E. A. Thompson, *Nottingham Medieval Studies*, 20 (1976), p. 4; S. I. Oost, *Galla Placidia* (Chicago, 1968), pp. 280–81.

22. J. Wacher, *Studies in the Archaeology and History of Cirencester*, pp. 16–17.

23. V. E. Nash-Williams, *Early Christian Monuments of Wales* (Cardiff, 1950), no. 92, 103; no. 104 is even dated by Justinus as consul (A.D. 540).

Table of Emperors

Constantine	306–37				
Constantine II	337–40	Magnentius	350–53		
Constans	337–50	Julian	361–63		
Constantius	337–61	Jovian	363–64		

East		*West*			
Valens	364–78	Valentinian I	364–75		
Theodosius I	379–95	Gratian	367–83		
		Valentinian II	383–92		
		Eugenius	392–94	(*Patricians or*	
		Theodosius I	394–95	*equivalent*)	
Arcadius	395–408	Honorius	395–423	(Stilicho	395–408)
				(Constantius	410–21)
Theodosius II	408–50	Valentinian III	425–55	(Aetius	433–54)
Marcian	450–57	Maximus	455–57		
Leo I	457–74	Majorian	457–61		
		Severus	461–67	(Ricimer	456–72)
		Anthemius	467–72		
		Olybrius	472–73		
Leo II	474	Glycerius	473–74		
Zeno	474–91	Julius Nepos	474–75		
		Romulus Augustulus	475–76	(Odoacer	476–93)

Abbreviations

Over the course of years I have come to recognize that the abundant use of abbreviations is more confusing to readers than helpful in saving space. A few very standard abbreviations as well as short titles for recent collections of essays, however, are listed below.

Assimilation	*Assimilation et résistance à la culture gréco-romaine dans le monde ancien,* ed. D. M. Pippidi (Bucharest/Paris, 1976).
Armées et fiscalité	*Armées et fiscalité dans le monde antique,* ed. A. Chastagnol, C. Nicolet, H. van Effenterre (Paris, 1977).
ANRW	*Aufstieg und Niedergang der römischen Welt,* ed. H. Temporini (Berlin, 1972–); begun as a tribute to Joseph Vogt this work has swelled into a huge number of volumes of specialized essays.
CIL	*Corpus Inscriptionum Latinarum* (Berlin, 1863–).
Dessau	Hermann Dessau, *Inscriptiones Latinae Selectae,* 3 vols. (Berlin, 1892–1916).
Les Dévaluations	*Les "Dévaluations" à Rome,* ed. G. Vallet (Rome, 1978).
Imperialism in the Ancient World	*Imperialism in the Ancient World,* ed. P. D. A. Garnsey and C. R. Whittaker (Cambridge, 1978).
PW	Pauly-Wissowa, *Real-Encyclopädie der classischen Altertumswissenschaft* (Stuttgart, 1893–).
Recherches sur les structures	*Recherches sur les structures sociales dans l'antiquité classique* (Paris, 1970).
SHA	*Scriptores Historiae Augustae.*

Bibliographical Note

Modern students of the Roman world have always worked most directly and comfortably from the literary evidence, including not only the ancient historians and biographers but also poetry, philosophical essays, legal commentaries, astrological treatises, and even dream handbooks; the range of these sources appears in the notes of this volume. But a great mass of inscriptions, papyri, coins, and physical remains also broadens our knowledge and often deepens it in areas which written works slight or ignore. For their use of this latter range of material three great scholars deserve mention: Theodor Mommsen, the driving force behind the publication of *Corpus Inscriptionum Latinarum* (1863 on); Harold Mattingly, who put the study of Roman imperial coinage on a solid base in *Coins of the Roman Empire in the British Museum* (1926 on); and M. I. Rostovtzeff, who showed in the text and plates of *The Social and Economic History of the Roman Empire* (1st ed. 1926; revised ed. 1957) how physical, especially archeological, evidence was valuable in its own right—a lesson which not all Roman historians have yet come to accept.

In the following bibliographical commentary I have generally limited citations to those works published in the past 30 years, and even in this span to those which have been most useful or have full bibliographies of their own. Not that the most recent discussion of any topic is necessarily the best, but it will lead the interested reader into earlier literature, which is so immense that any effort to encompass it would require volumes. Works cited in the notes are not always repeated here.

General

For individual events or persons one may turn to *The Oxford Classical Dictionary* (2d ed.; Oxford, 1970) or *Der Kleine Pauly*, 5 vols. (Stuttgart,

1964–75), both of which give brief bibliographies. The latest careful, annotated bibliography on the whole span of the Roman Empire is in Mason Hammond, *The City in the Ancient World* (Cambridge, Mass., 1972); in *Civilization and the Caesars: The Intellectual Revolution in the Roman Empire* (Ithaca, 1954; Norton reprint 1965) I gave a bibliography down into the early 1950s. For the first two centuries of the Empire see A. Garzetti, *From Tiberius to the Antonines* (London, 1974); F. Millar, *The Roman Empire and Its Neighbours* (London, 1967); and P. Petit, *Pax Romana* (Berkeley, 1976). For the later period see R. Rémondon, *La Crise de l'Empire romain de Marc-Aurèle à Anastase* (Paris, 1964); M. Grant, *The Climax of Empire* (London, 1968); A. H. M. Jones, *The Later Roman Empire 284–602* (Oxford, 1964). In "The History of the Roman Empire, 1911–1960," *Journal of Roman Studies*, 50 (1960), pp. 149–60 (now my *Collected Essays*, pp. 301–12), I gave some account of major trends in the study of the Empire and reached the unexpected conclusion that what was most necessary was not further exploration of social, intellectual, or religious developments but rather that "above all we desperately need a political history of the Roman Empire, which is solid and well-buttressed; which takes account of the detailed advance registered in epigraphic, numismatic, archaeological and other monographs; which is the product of a single individual's pen." This view, which has lain in the back of my mind, is the genesis of the present work. In "The Roman Place in History," the introductory essay in *ANRW*, 1 (Berlin, 1972), I also sought to explore the current dichotomy of scholarly views on which I commented more briefly in the Introduction to the present work.

Chapter I: Augustus

Among the latest or most useful discussions of Augustus' political position are P. Grenade, *Essai sur les origines du principat* (Paris, 1961); W. K. Lacey, "Octavian in the Senate, January 27, B.C.," *Journal of Roman Studies*, 64 (1974), pp. 176–84; F. de Martino, *Storia della costituzione romana*, 4. 1–2 (Naples, 1962); F. Millar, "Triumvirate and Principate," *Journal of Roman Studies*, 63 (1973), pp. 50–67; E. T. Salmon, "The Evolution of Augustus' Principate," *Historia*, 5 (1956), pp. 456–78. In "How Did Augustus Stop the Roman Revolution?" *Classical Journal*, 52 (1956), pp. 107–12 (now my *Collected Essays*, pp. 222–27) and more fully in *Civilization and the Caesars* I explored his outward respect for Republican theories and practical suppression of opposition. This interplay is the subject of a classic by Ronald Syme, *The Roman Revolution*

(Oxford, 1939), though its prosopographical approach and Tacitean style have both corrupted far too many younger and lesser Roman historians. C. Meier, *Res publica amissa* (Wiesbaden, 1966), is also a remarkable study of the forces at work in the Late Republic. P. Sattler, *Augustus und der Senat* (Göttingen, 1960), illuminates the degree of senatorial opposition which Augustus faced.

Roman concepts of "peace" and unending conquest are considered in P. A. Brunt, "Laus Imperii," *Imperialism in the Ancient World,* pp. 159–91; W. V. Harris, *War and Imperialism in Republican Rome, 327–70 B.C.* (Oxford, 1979), who argues for deliberate Roman expansion throughout this period; T. Hölscher, *Victoria Romana* (Mainz, 1967); S. Weinstock, "Pax and the 'Ara Pacis,'" *Journal of Roman Studies,* 50 (1960), pp. 44–58. Augustus' purported advice to Tiberius not to expand farther is given by Dio Cassius 56. 33; my student Josiah Ober is preparing a study which suggests that this represents only the view of Dio Cassius.

For Augustan wars see A. Brancati, *Augusto e la guerra di Spagna* (Urbino, 1963); R. Chevallier, *Rome et la Germanie au Ier siècle de notre ère* (Brussels, 1961); E. Demougeot, *La Formation de l'Europe et les invasions barbares,* 1 (Paris, 1969), pp. 69–114; C. M. Wells, *The German Policy of Augustus* (Oxford, 1972). H. D. Meyer, *Die Aussenpolitik des Augustus und die augusteische Dichtung* (Köln, 1961), is rightly criticized by P. A. Brunt, *Journal of Roman Studies,* 53 (1963), pp. 170–76.

In "Virgil's Acceptance of Octavian," *American Journal of Philology,* 76 (1955), pp. 34–46, and "Horace and Augustus," 90 (1969), pp. 58–64 (now in my *Essays on Ancient History,* pp. 228–47) I explored the attitudes of two major poets; see also A. La Penna, *Orazio e l'ideologia del principato* (Florence, 1963). E. Buchner's views on the Campus Martius have, as far as I know, only been reported in newspapers (as *Kölner Stadt-Anzeiger,* August 11, 1980); see earlier H. T. Rowell, "The Forum and Funeral *Imagines* of Augustus," *Memoirs of the American Academy in Rome,* 17 (1940), pp. 131–43.

The imperial cult continues to receive attention; see recently *Le Culte des souverains dans l'Empire romain* (Entretiens Hardt 19, 1973); A. Wlosok, ed., *Römischer Kaiserkult* (Darmstadt, 1978); the brief but wise remarks of W. den Boer, *Entretiens Hardt,* 26 (1980), pp. 36ff. S. R. F. Price, "Between Man and God," *Journal of Roman Studies,* 80 (1980), pp. 28–43, makes the very important point that most sacrifices were on behalf of the ruler, not to him.

Augustus' attitude toward the Greek East is treated by G. W. Bowersock, *Augustus and the Greek World* (Oxford, 1963); and J. A. O. Larsen, "The Policy of Augustus in Greece," *Acta classica*, 1 (1958), pp. 123–30.

P. A. Brunt and J. M. Moore have edited *Res Gestae Divi Augusti* (Oxford, 1967); his legislation is reconstructed in S. Riccobono, ed., *Acta divi Augusti*, 1 (Paris, 1945); R. Syme, *History in Ovid* (Oxford, 1978), is the latest study of that unfortunate poet. Before turning to the output of a tremendous variety of popular works on the ancient world M. Grant wrote *From Imperium to Auctoritas* (corr. ed., Oxford, 1969), and *Six Main Aes Coinages of Augustus* (Edinburgh, 1953), which suggest the wealth of information to be gained from coinage.

Chapter II: The Imperial Succession

Legal and practical problems involved in imperial succession are discussed by J. Béranger, *Principatus* (Geneva, 1973); M. Hammond, "The Transmission of the Powers of the Roman Emperor," *Memoirs of the American Academy in Rome*, 24 (1956); B. Parsi, *Désignation et investiture de l'empereur romain (Ier–IIe siècle après J.-C.)* (Paris, 1962); M. H. Prévost, *Les Adoptions politiques à Rome sous la République et le Principat* (Paris, 1949), who stresses the inheritance of a *clientela* via adoption; D. Timpe, *Untersuchungen zur Kontinuität des frühen Prinzipats (Historia Einzelschriften*, 5 [1962]).

Theodor Mommsen, *Römisches Staatsrecht*, 2 (3d ed.; Leipzig, 1887), p. 133, summed up his view of the imperial position as "eine durch der rechtlich permanente Revolution temperierte Autokratie," a view glossed by A. Heuss, *ANRW*, 2. 1 (1974), pp. 77–90. Among many other treatments see M. Hammond, *The Antonine Monarchy* (Rome, 1959); E. Meyer, *Römischer Staat und Staatsgedanke* (3d ed.; Zürich, 1964), pp. 360ff.; F. de Martino, *Storia della costituzione romana*, 4–5 (Naples, 1962–71).

Major elements involved in imperial survival will be treated in following chapters; but for the senatorial aristocracy see A. Bergener, *Die führende Senatorenschicht im frühen Prinzipat (14 bis 68 n. Chr.)* (Bonn, 1965), and on philosophic opposition under the Flavians my *Civilization and the Caesars,* Ch. VII, and Ramsay MacMullen, *Enemies of the Roman Order* (Cambridge, Mass., 1966), pp. 32ff. Tacitus, *Histories* 1. 15–16 is a key passage in the theory of adoption; but the historian's friend Pliny the Younger (*Panegyric* 94. 5) expected a son to be born to Trajan and succeed him! Oaths to the emperor, taken by all elements at various times, are well treated by P. Herrmann, *Der römische Kaisereid* (Göttingen, 1968).

The place of the *populus Romanus* is surveyed by T. W. Africa, "Urban Violence in Imperial Rome," *Journal of Interdisciplinary History*, 2 (1971), pp. 3–21; B. Baldwin, "Rulers and Ruled at Rome: A.D. 14–192," *Ancient Society*, 4 (1973), pp. 149–63; Z. Yavetz, *Plebs and Princeps* (New York, 1969).

L. Wickert, *s.v.* "Princeps," PW 22. 2 (1954), has a list of 41 adjectives and 38 nouns describing imperial virtues in propaganda; Mattingly's introduction to successive volumes of *Coins of the Roman Empire in the British Museum* sensitively explore the patterns of programs placed before the public by this means (with more general and thoughtful comments in *The Man in the Roman Street* [New York, 1966]); M. Amit, "Propagande de succès et d'euphorie dans l'Empire romain," *Iura*, 16 (1965), pp. 52–75, gives a brief collection. C. H. V. Sutherland, *The Emperor and the Coinage* (London, 1976), discusses the manner in which numismatic programs were established. On liberty see G. Walser, "Der Kaiser als Vindex Libertatis," *Historia*, 4 (1955), pp. 353–67; C. Wirszubski, *Libertas as a Political Idea at Rome during the Late Republic and Early Principate* (London, 1950); my "Perfect Democracy of the Roman Empire," *American Historical Review*, 58 (1952), pp. 1–16 (now in my *Collected Essays*, pp. 262–77).

For Vespasian himself, see A. Ferrill, "Otho, Vitellius, and the Propaganda of Vespasian," *Classical Journal*, 60 (1965), pp. 267–69; J. Gagé, "Vespasien et la mémoire de Galba," *Revue des études anciennes*, 54 (1952), pp. 290–315; A. Henrichs, "Vespasian's Visit to Alexandria," *Zeitschrift für Papyrologie und Epigraphik*, 3 (1968), pp. 51–80; P. Fouad 8 (R. Merkelbach, *Archiv für Papyrusforschung*, 16 [1956], p. 111).

Tiberius' accession has recently been discussed by D. Flach, "Der Regierungsanfang des Tiberius," *Historia*, 22 (1973), pp. 552–69; H. H. Schmitt, "Der pannonische Aufstand des Jahres 14 n. Chr. und der Regierungsantritt des Tiberius," *Historia*, 7 (1958), pp. 378–83.

Chapter III: The Roman Aristocracy

On the role of the Senate see the works listed above for Chapter II (Bergener et al.) and also for the reign of Tiberius H. W. Bird, "L. Aelius Seianus and His Political Significance," *Latomus*, 28 (1969), pp. 61–98; A. Boddington, "Sejanus: Whose Conspiracy?" *American Journal of Philology*, 84 (1963), pp. 1–16. The futile meeting of the Senate after the murder of Gaius is magnificently portrayed by Josephus, *Antiquities of the Jews,* book 19. Factionalism under Nero is demonstrated by B. Baldwin, "Executions, Trials and Punishments in the Reign of Nero," *Parola del Passato,* 22 (1967), pp. 425–39. H. G. Pflaum, *Les Procurateurs équestres sous le Haut-Empire romain* (Paris, 1950), pp. 206–8, finds camarillas under Claudius and Nero; R. Syme, *Tacitus* (Oxford, 1958), pp. 601ff., under Trajan (but cf. Z. Rubin, *Journal of Roman Studies,* 64 [1974], p. 232); Birley, *Septimius Severus,* Appendix III, under that ruler (doubted by T. D. Barnes, *Historia,* 16 [1967], p. 107).

On the senatorial nobility see recently J. Gagé, *Les Classes sociales dans l'Empire romain* (Paris, 1964); K. Hopkins, "Elite Mobility in the Roman Empire," *Past and Present,* 32 (1965), pp. 12–26; B. Levick, "Imperial Control of the Elections under the Early Principate," *Historia,* 16 (1967), pp. 207–30; H. W. Pleket, "Sociale stratificatie en sociale mobiliteit in de Romeinse Keizertijd," *Tijdschrift voor Geschiedenis,* 84 (1971), pp. 215–51. P. Garnsey, *Studies in Roman Property,* ed. M. I. Finley (Cambridge, 1976), pp. 123–36, argues aristocrats derived as much income from urban shops and tenements as rural estate (urban property included brothels [*Digest* 5. 3. 27. 1]); Bruce Frier, *Landlords and Tenants in Imperial Rome* (Princeton, 1980), pp. 21–26, is more cautious.

Public careers are considered in too schematic fashion by E. Birley, "Senators in the Emperor's Service," *Proceedings of the British Academy,* 39 (1954), pp. 197–214, and "Beförderungen und Versetzungen im römischen Heere," *Carnuntum-Jahrbuch,* 1957, pp. 3–20 (note the scepticism of B. Campbell, *Journal of Roman Studies,* 65 [1975], p. 18). R. D. Saller, "Promotion and Patronage in Equestrian Careers," *Journal of Roman Studies,* 70 (1980), pp. 44–59, also discounts Pflaum's patterns of advancement.

On equestrians see the works of Pflaum listed for the next chapter and also S. J. de Laet, "La composition de l'ordre équestre sous Auguste et Tibère," *Revue belge de philologie et d'histoire,* 20 (1941), pp. 509–31; T. P. Wiseman, "The Definition of 'Equus Romanus' in the Late Republic and Early Empire," *Historia,* 19 (1970), pp. 67–83.

Legal distinctions are well surveyed by P. Garnsey, *Social Status and Legal Privilege in the Roman Empire* (Oxford, 1970); see also H. G. Pflaum, "Titulature et rang social durant le Haut-empire," *Recherches sur les structures,* pp. 159–85; M. Reinhold, "Usurpation of Status and Status Symbols in the Roman Empire," *Historia,* 20 (1971), pp. 273–302; R. MacMullen, *Roman Social Relations 50 B.C. to A.D. 284* (New

Haven, 1974). The term *vir clarissimus* appears already in A.D. 56 (Dessau 6043).

Chapter IV: Governing the Empire

On the determination of policy see J. A. Crook, *Consilium Principis* (Cambridge, 1955); G. G. Tissani, "Sul 'consilium principis' in età trainea," *Studia et documenta historiae et iuris,* 31 (1965), pp. 222–45; and the efforts to find factions noted above for Chapter III. The central machinery was studied by W. L. Wannemacher, "The Development of Imperial Civil Officia During the Principate," Ph.D. Michigan 1940; specific offices by H. Pavis d'Escurac, *Le Préfecture de l'annone* (Paris, 1976); S. J. de Laet, *Portorium* (Bruges, 1949); G. Rickman, *The Corn Supply of Ancient Rome* (Oxford, 1980).

Levels of personnel and careers can be found in P. R. C. Weaver, *Familia Caesaris* (Cambridge, 1972), and his article "Freedmen Procurators in the Imperial Administration," *Historia,* 14 (1966), pp. 460–69; G. Boulvert, *Esclaves et affranchis impériaux sous le Haut-Empire romain* (Naples, 1970) and *Domestique et fonctionnaire sous le Haut-Empire romain* (Paris, 1974). On equestrians see H. G. Pflaum, *Les Procurateurs équestres sous le Haut-Empire romain* (Paris, 1950), and *Les Carrières procuratoriennes équestres sous le Haut-Empire romain,* 3 vols. (Paris, 1960–61); R. P. Saller, "Promotion and Patronage in Equestrian Careers," *Journal of Roman Studies,* 70 (1980), pp. 44–63; A. N. Sherwin-White, "Procurator Augusti," *Papers of the British School at Rome,* 15 (1938), pp. 11–26. Senators are discussed by E. Birley, "Inscriptions Indicative of Impending or Recent Movements," *Chiron,* 9 (1979), pp. 495–505; J. Fitz, *Die Laufbahn der Staathalter in der römischen Provinz Moesia Inferior* (Weimar, 1966); R. Sherk, "Specialization in the Provinces of Germany," *Historia,* 20 (1971), pp. 110–21. On legal training see H. I. Marrou, *A History of Education in Antiquity* (New York, 1956), pp. 387ff.; D. Liebs, *ANRW,* 2. 15 (1976), pp. 197–286, with full bibliography.

G. H. Stevenson, *Roman Provincial Administration till the Antonines* (Oxford, 1939), has an old-fashioned air of a paean to Roman peace similar to praises of British imperialism; on taxation see M. Corbier, "Dévaluations et fiscalité," *Les Dévaluations,* pp. 273–301, and A. H. M. Jones, *The Ancient Economy* (Oxford, 1974). The meager evidence for local collection is noted by Jones, p. 165 n. 83, 180–83; *Inscriptiones Graecae* 5, 1, 1432–33, illustrates the procedure in Messene. Bibliography on centuriation is given by R. Chevallier, *ANRW,* 2. 1, pp. 767–70, and A. W. Dilke, pp. 564–92; the latter has also written *The Roman Land Surveyors* (New York, 1973).

Varying opinions over the meaning of the term *fiscus*, which can connote purely private income and also state treasuries in the provinces and Rome, have been presented by F. Millar, *Journal of Roman Studies*, 53 (1963), pp. 29–42; P. A. Brunt, *Journal of Roman Studies*, 56 (1966), pp. 75–91; and A. N. Sherwin-White, *The Letters of Pliny* (Oxford, 1966), p. 562, who properly refers back to A. H. M. Jones' discussion in *Journal of Roman Studies*, 40 (1950), pp. 22–29 (now in *Studies in Roman Government and Law* [Oxford, 1960], pp. 101–14). See also H. Nesselhauf, "Patrimonium und res privata des römischen Kaisers," *Antiquitas*, ser. 4, 2 (1964), pp. 73–93.

On jurisdiction see J. Bleicken, *Senatsgericht und Kaisergericht* (Göttingen, 1962); A. H. M. Jones, "Imperial and Senatorial Jurisdiction," *Studies in Roman Government and Law*, pp. 69–98; J. M. Kelly, *Princeps judex* (Weimar, 1957); S. J. de Laet, "Où en est le problème de la jurisdiction impériale?" *Antiquité classique*, 14 (1945), pp. 145–63. On the provincial level: G. P. Burton, "Proconsuls, Assizes and the Administration of Justice Under the Empire," *Journal of Roman Studies*, 65 (1975), pp. 92–106; P. Garnsey, "The Criminal Jurisdiction of Governors," *Journal of Roman Studies*, 58 (1968), pp. 51–59; A. H. M. Jones, "Appeal unto Caesar," *Studies in Roman Government and Law*, pp. 53–65. Procuratorial jurisdiction is a debatable matter; see D. Stockton, *Historia*, 10 (1961), pp. 116–20, and F. Millar, *Historia*, 13 (1964), pp. 180–87, and 14 (1965), pp. 363–67; P. A. Brunt, *Latomus*, 25 (1966), pp. 461–89. R. W. Davies, *Ancient Society*, 4 (1973), pp. 199–212, notices soldiers as judges.

Chapter V: The Cities of the Empire

R. Chevallier, *ANRW*, 2. 1, pp. 649–788, and Hammond, *City in the Ancient World,* give full bibliographies; the first chapter of Edith Ennen, *The Medieval Town* (New York, 1979), is an excellent analysis of the major characteristics of an ancient city.

Localism is treated in many essays in *Assimilation;* P. A. Brunt, "The Revolt of Vindex and the Fall of Nero," *Latomus,* 18 (1959), pp. 531–59; R. MacMullen, "Nationalism in Roman Egypt," *Aegyptus,* 44 (1964), pp. 179–99, "The Celtic Renaissance," *Historia,* 14 (1965), pp. 93–104, and *Enemies of the Roman Order* (Cambridge, Mass., 1966), pp. 215ff.; F. Millar, "Local Cultures in the Roman Empire: Libyan, Punic and Latin in Roman Africa," *Journal of Roman Studies,* 58 (1968), pp. 126–

34; *Die Sprachen im römischen Reich der Kaiserzeit,* ed. G. Neumann (*Bonner Jahrbücher,* Beiheft 40 [1980]); A. N. Sherwin-White, *The Roman Citizenship* (2d ed.; Oxford, 1973), pp. 419–22.

For peasants see P. Garnsey, "Peasants in Ancient Roman Society," *Journal of Peasant Studies,* 3 (1976), pp. 221–35; R. MacMullen, "Peasants during the Principate," *ANRW,* 2. 1, pp. 253–61; G. C. Picard, "Observations sur la condition des populations rurales dans l'Empire romain, en Gaule et en Africa," *ANRW,* 2. 3, pp. 98–111. These as well as K. D. White, *Roman Farming* (Ithaca, 1970) and V. A. Sirago, *L'Italia agraria sotto Traiano* (Louvain, 1958), touch on the shift from rural slavery toward free tenants. On slavery it will suffice to cite M. I. Finley, *Ancient Slavery and Modern Ideology* (New York, 1980), with full bibliography; to give one example of the decline even in the cities, over one third of the inscriptions of Salona are of slaves and freedmen down to the mid-second century, but by the last decades are only one in ten (J. J. Wilkes, *Dalmatia* [London, 1969], p. 234).

Local aristocrats are considered by M. G. Jarrett, *Historia,* 12 (1963), pp. 209ff., in Africa; Wilkes, *Dalmatia,* pp. 240, 303, 316, 336, for that province; J. A. O. Larsen, *Classical Philology,* 48 (1953), pp. 86–94, in Greece; S. Mitchell, *Journal of Roman Studies,* 64 (1974), pp. 27–39, and W. M. Ramsay, *The Social Basis of Roman Power in Asia Minor* (Aberdeen, 1941)—an unfortunately truncated work—in Asia Minor. The powerful role of Alexandrian upper classes in influencing a governor is illustrated by Philo, *In Flaccum.*

On the problem of Romanization in the east see J. H. Oliver's edition of Aelius Aristides, *On Rome* (*Transactions of the American Philosophical Society,* n. s., 43. 4 [1953]), and H. Bengtson, "Das Imperium Romanum im griechischer Sicht," *Gymnasium,* 71 (1964), pp. 160–66; P. A. Brunt, *Assimilation,* pp. 161–73; B. Forte, *Rome and the Romans as the Greeks Saw Them* (Rome, 1972); A. H. M. Jones, *The Ancient Economy* (Oxford, 1974), pp. 90–113; J. Palm, *Rom, Römertum und Imperium in der griechischen Literatur der Kaiserzeit* (Lund, 1959).

In the west, see M. Bénabou, *La Résistance africaine à la Romanisation* (Paris, 1976), and his essay in *Assimilation,* pp. 367–75; S. Dyson, "Native Revolts in the Roman Empire," *Historia,* 20 (1971), pp. 239–74, and his review of the topic in *ANRW,* 2. 3, pp. 138–75; P. D. A. Garnsey, "Rome's African Empire under the Principate," *Imperialism in the Ancient World,* pp. 223–54; P. Lambrechts, *De geestelijke Weerstand van de westelijke Provincies tegen Rome* (Brussels, 1966), which is concerned more with a later period; D. Nörr, *Imperium und Polis in der hohen Prinzipatszeit* (Munich, 1966), pp. 85–93; Sherwin-White, *Roman*

Citizenship, part III, who gave a reasoned view over 40 years ago which still appears valid; and his more recent *Racial Prejudice in Imperial Rome* (Cambridge, 1967). On the case of Tertullian see T. D. Barnes, *Tertullian* (Oxford, 1971), pp. 110–11; R. Klein, *Tertullian und das römisches Reich* (Heidelberg, 1968); Sherwin-White, *Roman Citizenship,* pp. 433–37; C. Guignebert, *Tertullien, Etude sur les sentiments à l'égard de l'Empire* (Paris, 1901), is still sound.

J. H. D'Arms, "Puteoli in the Second Century of the Roman Empire," *Journal of Roman Studies,* 64 (1974), pp. 104–24, and "The Status of Traders in the Roman World," *Ancient and Modern* (Ann Arbor, 1977), pp. 159–80, illuminates the role of urban upper classes in trade. Beyond the masterful study of Rostovtzeff see more recently R. Duncan-Jones, *The Economy of the Roman Empire* (Cambridge, 1974); M. I. Finley, *The Ancient Economy* (Berkeley, 1973); J. Rougé, *Recherches sur l'organisation du commerce maritime en Méditerranée sous l'Empire romain* (Paris, 1966); A. H. M. Jones, *Ancient Economy,* pp. 35–60; J. H. D'Arms and E. C. Knopff, ed., *The Seaborne Commerce of Ancient Rome* (Rome, 1980). K. Hopkins, "Economic Growth and Towns in Classical Antiquity," *Towns in Societies,* ed. Abrams and Wrigley (Cambridge, 1978), pp. 35–77, is a valuable essay reflected at several points in my text. H. J. Eggers, *Der römischen Import im freien Germanien* (Hamburg, 1951), and R. E. M. Wheeler, *Rome beyond the Imperial Frontiers* (London, 1954), discuss external trade.

Chapter VI: Army, Roads, and Frontiers

Recent general studies of the Roman army include G. R. Watson, *The Roman Soldier* (Ithaca, 1969), and G. Webster, *The Roman Army of the First and Second Centuries A. D.* (2d ed.; London, 1979). *ANRW,* 2. 1, contains a number of essays, including R. W. Davies, "The Daily Life of the Roman Soldier under the Principate," pp. 299–338. See also his essay, "The Investigation of Some Crimes in Roman Egypt," *Ancient Society,* 4 (1973), pp. 199–212; B. Dobson, "The Centurion and Social Mobility during the Principate," *Recherches sur les structures sociales,* pp. 99–116; and *Die Primipilares* (Köln, 1978); P. A. Holder, *The Auxilia from Augustus to Trajan,* British Archaeological Reports, Suppl. ser. 70 (1980), a purely factual study. In Chapters III and IV senatorial and equestrian careers have been noted, and pay in the Appendix to Chapter IV; see also G. Alföldy, "Die Generalität des römischen Heeres," *Bonner Jahrbücher,* 169 (1969), pp. 233–46.

Recruitment is discussed by P. A. Brunt, "Conscription and Volunteering in the Roman Imperial Army," *Scripta Classica Israelitica*, 1 (1974), pp. 90–115, and "C. Fabricius Priscus and an Augustan Dilectus," *Zeitschrift für Papyriologie und Epigraphik*, 13 (1974), pp. 161–85; R. W. Davies, "Joining the Roman Army," *Bonner Jahrbücher*, 169 (1969), pp. 208–32; G. Forni, *Il Reclutamento delle legioni da Augusto à Diocleziano* (Milan, 1953), and in *ANRW*, 2. 1, pp. 339–91; J. F. Gilliam, "Enrollment in the Roman Imperial Army," *Eos*, 48. 2 (1957), pp. 207–16; J. C. Mann, "The Raising of New Legions during the Principate," *Hermes*, 91 (1963), pp. 483–89. Religious calendars are best exemplified by the Feriale Duranum (Fink, *Roman Military Records*, no. 117).

For roads and travel see L. Casson, *Travel in the Ancient World* (Toronto, 1974); the works by Chevallier and Pekáry cited in notes; the bibliography of H. E. Herzig, *ANRW*, 2. 1, pp. 593–648; and on the post H. G. Pflaum, *Memoires de l'Académie des Inscriptions et Belles-Lettres*, 14 (1940), pp. 189ff. *CIL* 3.6123=14207[34] has the phrase *vias militares*.

Native revolts are treated by S. Dyson in two articles listed above for Chapter V; see also M. Rachet, *Rome et les Berberes* (Brussels, 1970), and G. Webster, *Boudica* (London, 1978). Recent work on the Jews includes E. M. Smallwood, *The Jews in the Roman World* (Leiden, 1976), who does not accept (pp. 546–7) Eck's firmly argued date of 74 for Masada; N. R. M. de Lange, "Jewish Attitudes to the Roman Empire," *Imperialism in the Ancient World*, pp. 255–81; Y. Yadin, *Masada* (New York, 1966).

For frontiers and frontier wars see A. R. Birley, "Roman Frontiers and Roman Frontier Policy," *Transactions of the Architectural and Archaeological Society of Durham and Northumberland*, n. s. 3 (1974), pp. 13–25; Demougeot, *La Formation de l'Europe*, 1, pp. 114–256; D. R. Dudley and G. Webster, *The Roman Conquest of Britain A.D. 43–57* (London, 1965); J. C. Mann, "The Frontiers of the Principate," *ANRW*, 2, 1, pp. 508–33; H. Petrikovits, *Das römische Rheinland* (Köln, 1960); H. Schönberger, "The Roman Frontier in Germany," *Journal of Roman Studies*, 59 (1969), pp. 144–97; K. H. Ziegler, *Die Beziehungen zwischen Rom und dem Partherreich* (Wiesbaden, 1964).

E. Gren, *Kleinasien und Ostbalkan in der wirtschaftlichen Entwicklung der römischen Kaiserzeit* (Uppsale, 1941), drew attention to the economic importance of the stationing of the Roman army on the frontier; see more recently especially K. Hopkins, *Journal of Roman Studies*, 70 (1980), pp. 101ff., and compare the role of military expenditure in promoting late medieval economic activity, A. Murray, *Reason and Society in the Middle Ages* (Oxford, 1978), pp. 82–84.

Chapter VII: The First Test

Beyond my discussion in *Civilization and the Caesars* P. Brown, *The World of Late Antiquity from Marcus Aurelius to Muhammad* (London, 1971), and M. Grant, *The Climax of Rome* (London, 1968), survey the great intellectual and spiritual changes in the third and fourth centuries; architectural and sculptural aspects are discussed by R. Brilliant, *The Arch of Septimius Severus in the Roman Forum* (Rome, 1967), and *Gesture and Rank in Roman Art* (*Memoirs of the Connecticut Academy of Arts and Sciences,* 14 [1963]); and W. MacDonald, *The Architecture of the Roman Empire,* 1 (New Haven, 1965), on the Pantheon.

R. MacMullen, *Roman Government's Response to Crisis, A.D. 235– 337* (New Haven, 1976), and M. Mazza, *Lotte sociali e restaurazione autoritaria nel 3. secolo d. C.* (Catania, 1970), complement each other, MacMullen citing especially sources and Mazza a wealth of modern studies. An earlier bibliography is in T. Pekáry, *Die Krise des römischen Reiches* (Berlin, 1962). See also P. Oliva, *Pannonia and the Onset of Crisis in the Roman Empire* (Prague, 1962).

For the Severi see G. Barbieri, "Aspetti della politica di Settimio Severo," *Epigraphica,* 14 (1952), pp. 3–48; A. Birley, *Septimius Severus, The African Emperor* (Garden City, 1972); A. Calderini, *I Severi* (Bologna, 1949). For senatorial opposition to Maximinus and the Gordians see K. Dietz, *"Senatus contra principem"* (*Vestigia* 29; Munich, 1980); J. Gagé, "Les Organisations de 'Iuvenes' en Italie et en Afrique du début du IIIe siècle au 'bellum Aquiliense,' 238 ap. J.-C.," *Historia,* 19 (1970), pp. 232–57; F. Kolb, "Der Aufstand der Provinz Africa Proconsularis im Jahr 238 n. Chr.," *Historia,* 26 (1977), pp. 440–77; T. Spagnuolo Vigorita, *Secta temporum meorum* (Palermo, 1978). Peculiarly enough there are more milestones of Gordian III from Britain and many other provinces than any other ruler down to Constantine and also a remarkable number of official bust types (S. Ward, *American Journal of Archaeology,* 85 [1981], pp. 62–63). Gallienus is considered by L. de Blois, *The Policy of the Emperor Gallienus* (Beiden, 1971).

On military problems see Demougeot, *La Formation de l'Europe,* 1, pp. 389–552; J. Fitz, "Die Vereinigung der Donauprovinzen in der Mitte des 3. Jahrhunderts," *Studien zu den Militärgrenzen Roms* (Köln/Graz, 1967), pp. 113ff.; Luttwak, *Grand Strategy,* ch. 3; F. Millar, "P. Herennius Dexippus," *Journal of Roman Studies,* 59 (1969), pp. 12–29; H. von Petrikovits, "Fortifications in the North-Western Roman Empire from the Third to the Fifth Centuries A.D.," *Journal of Roman Studies,* 61 (1971), pp. 178–218; R. Saxer, *Untersuchungen zu den Vexillationen des römischen Kaiserheeres von Augustus bis Diokletian* (Köln, 1967). E. Birley, "Septimius Severus and the Roman Army," *Epigraphische Studien,* 8 (1963), pp. 63–82, showed the nucleus of a field force was already then existent and can indeed even be traced back to Marcus Aurelius.

Financial problems are treated by A. K. Bowman, "The Crown-tax in Roman Egypt," *Bulletin of the American Society of Papyrologists,* 4 (1967), pp. 59–74; J. P. Callu, *La Politique Monétaire des empereurs romains de 238 à 311* (Paris, 1969); T. Pekáry, "Studien zur römischen Währungs- und Finanzgeschichte von 161 bis 235 n. Chr.," *Historia,* 8 (1958), pp. 443–89; J. Szilagyi, "Prices and Wages in the Western Provinces of the Roman Empire," *Acta antiqua academiae Hungaricae,* 6 (1963), pp. 325–90. T. B. Jones surveyed the mints of Asia Minor in *Proceedings of the American Philosophical Society,* 107 (1963). The argument of D. van Berchem, *L'Annona militaire* (Paris, 1937), has not been generally accepted.

For cities see P. Garnsey, "Aspects of the Decline of the Urban Aristocracy in the Empire," *ANRW,* 2. 1, pp. 229–52; D. Nörr, "Origo," *Tijdschrift voor Rechtsgeschiedenis,* 31 (1963), pp. 525–600; and *Imperium und Polis in der Hohen Prinzipatszeit* (Munich, 1966); E. Will, "Recherches sur le développement urbain sous l'Empire romain dans le Nord de la France," *Gallia,* 20 (1962), pp. 79–101.

Diocletian does not have an adequate biography in any language; see for him and Constantine A. Alföldi, *Die monarchische Repräsentation im römischen Kaiserreich* (Darmstadt, 1977); P. Bruun, "The Successive Monetary Reforms of Diocletian," *Museum Notes of the American Numismatic Society,* 24 (1979), pp. 129–48; J.-P. Callu, "Denier et nummus (300–354)," *Les Dévaluations,* pp. 107–21; A. Cerati, *Caractère annonaire et assiette de l'impôt foncier au Bas-Empire* (Paris, 1975); S. Lauffer, *Diokletians Preisedikt* (Berlin, 1971); W. Seston, *Dioclétien et la tétrarchie* (Paris, 1946); D. van Berchem, *L'Armee de Dioclétien et la réforme constantienne* (Paris, 1952): R. MacMullen, *Soldier and Civilian in the Later Roman Empire* (Cambridge, Mass., 1963).

Chapter VIII: The Final Test

Beyond works on the Later Empire cited at the beginning of this Bibliographical Note see A. Chastagnol, *Le Sénat romain sous le règne d'Odoacre* (Paris, 1966), and *La Préfecture urbaine à Rome sous le Bas-Empire* (Paris, 1960); W. Ensslin, *Theoderich der Grosse* (2d ed.; Munich, 1959); J. Matthews, *Western Aristocracies and Imperial Court, A.D. 364–425* (Oxford, 1975), a very valuable study; S. Mazzarino, *Aspetti sociali del quarto secolo* (Rome, 1951); M. A. Wes, *Das Ende des Kaisertums im Westen des römischen Reiches* (The Hague, 1967). On the continuity in the Gallic nobility see M. Heinzelmann, *Bischofsherrschaft in Gallien* (Munich, 1976), and earlier K. F. Stroheker, *Der senatorische Adel im spätantiken Gallien* (Tübingen, 1948). K. Hopkins, "Elite Mobility in the Roman Empire," *Past and Present,* no. 32 (1962), 12–26, and "Social Mobility in the Late Roman Empire," *Classical Quarterly,* 2. ser., 11 (1968), pp. 239–49; R. MacMullen, "Social Mobility and the Theodosian Code," *Journal of Roman Studies,* 54 (1964), pp. 49–53; A. H. M. Jones, *The Conflict between Paganism and Christianity in the Fourth Century,* ed. A. Momigliano (Oxford, 1963), pp. 17–37 all consider variety of mobility.

Economic changes are discussed by A. Bernardi, "The Economic Problems of the Roman Empire at the Time of Its Decline," *Studia et documenta historiae et iuris,* 31 (1965), pp. 110–70; M. Fulford, "Coin Circulation and Mint Activity in the Late Roman Empire," *Archaeological Journal,* 135 (1978), pp. 67–114; L. Ruggini, *Economia e società nell' Italia annonaria* (Milan, 1961). For the cities see R. Ganghoffer, *L'Evolution des institutions municipales en Occident et en Orient au Bas-Empire* (Paris, 1963); G. Fasoli, *La città medievale italiana* (Florence, 1973), pp. 7–23 (which I know through the courtesy of my colleague Marvin Becker), is schematic and unpersuasive as against E. Ennen, *The Medieval Town* (New York, 1979), J. Percival, *The Roman Villa* (London, 1976), and G. A. Mansuelli, *Le ville nel mondo romano* (Milan, 1958), discuss the changes in rural life; on other aspects see L. Harmand, *Le Patronat sur les collectivités publiques* (Paris, 1957); C. R. Whittaker, "Agri deserti," *Studies in Roman Property,* ed. M. I. Finley (Cambridge, 1976), pp. 137–65; R. van Dann, "Heretics, Bandits and Bishops" (Cambridge Ph.D. thesis, 1974) apparently argues that the Bagaudae were led by local lords to gain power rather than struggles of peasants against patrons as usually put (E. M. Wightman, *American Journal of Ancient History,* 3 [1978], p. 111).

The invasions have been much treated; see P. Courcelle, *Histoire littéraire des grandes invasions germaniques* (Paris, 1948); Demougeot, *La Formation de l'Europe* 2. 2 (Paris, 1979); D. Hoffmann, *Das spätrömische Bewegungsheer und die Notitia Dignitatum* (Düsseldorf, 1967–70); E. A. Thompson, "The End of Roman Spain," *Nottingham Medieval Studies,* 20 (1976) and successive volumes, which is to be published by the University of Wisconsin Press.

My picture of Roman Britain is based on M. W. Barley and R. P. C. Hanson, eds., *Christianity in Britain 300–700* (Leicester, 1968); *The End of Roman Britain,* ed. P. J. Casey, British Archaeological Reports, British Series, 71 (1979); J. Morris, *The Age of Arthur* (New York, 1973); P. H. Sawyer, *From Roman Britain to Norman England* (New York, 1978); A. L. F. Rivet, *The Roman Villa in Britain* (London, 1969). H. P. R. Finberg, *Roman and Saxon Withington: A Study in Continuity* (Leicester, 1959), cited in R. Reece, *Studies in the Archaeology and History of Cirencester,* p. 71 (itself a remarkable critique), seeks to show agricultural continuity in one locality. Twenty-five Roman coins have recently turned up at a purely Saxon site (*The Saxon and Medieval Palaces at Cheddar: Excavations 1960–62* ed. P. Rahtz [British Archaeological Reports, British Series, 65 (1979), pp. 288–91]), but G. C. Boon explains these as curiosities, counters, or weights; Saxons are not permitted to have any interest in coins. Many other valuable works could be cited; the publication of books on Roman Britain is a vigorous industry.

Index

DATE DUE

The Roman Empire—stretching from Scotland to Egypt, from the Euphrates River to the Atlantic Ocean—flourished for five hundred years. Although its decline and fall are much studied, less often considered are the factors that contributed to this remarkable longevity, a survival that defied all geographical, economic, and political odds.

In this probing study, Starr covers the whole sweep of imperial history, analyzing the binding forces of government and the army as initiated by Augustus, the maturing of these forces under subsequent emperors, and the eventual collapse of this network in the western provinces. Also examined are the issues of economic stagnation, intellectual revival, the rise of Christianity, and the effects of romanization on conquered peoples. Not simply a chronological summary, the book explores in piquant, telling detail the elements and institutions that shaped the Empire's history. An extensive annotated bibliography of relevant, modern literature enhances the text.

"A masterly synthesis of high clarity and dramatic intensity.... Professor Starr's book is a superbly controlled and structured distillation of a lifetime of research, meditation, and teaching....It will long be read with profit by students and the general public."
—**Meyer Reinhold,** University of Missouri, Columbia

The Author

Chester G. Starr, Bentley Professor of History, University of Michigan, is author of many books including *The Ancient Greeks* (1971), *The Ancient Romans* (1971), *Early Man* (1973), *The Economic and Social Growth of Early Greece, 800-500 B.C.* (1977), and *A History of the Ancient World,* Third Edition (1983), all published by Oxford.

Oxford University Press, New York

Cover design by Egon Lauterberg   ISBN 0-19-503130-X
Cover photo: courtesy of National Parks Commission, copyright H.M. Government, United Kingdom.